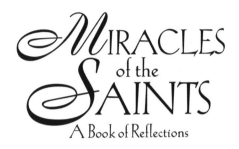

MIRACLES of the SAINTS

A Book of Reflections

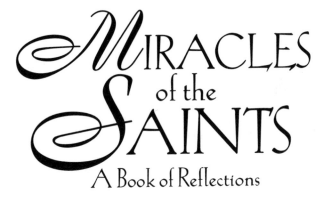

MIRACLES of the SAINTS

A Book of Reflections

True Stories of Lives Touched by the Supernatural

BERT GHEZZI

The Marian Center
of Springfield
313 EAST MONROE
SPRINGFIELD, IL 62701
(217) 744-3610

ZondervanPublishingHouse
Grand Rapids, Michigan

A Division of HarperCollins*Publishers*

Miracles of the Saints
Copyright © 1996 by Bert Ghezzi

Requests for information should be addressed to:

⚒ ZondervanPublishingHouse
Grand Rapids, Michigan 49530

Library of Congress Cataloging-in-Publication Data

Ghezzi, Bert.
    Miracles of the saints: true stories of lives touched by the supernatural / Bert
Ghezzi.
        p.   cm.
    Includes bibliographical references (p.   ) and index.
    ISBN: 0–310–20700-2
    1. Christian saints—Biography.   2. Miracles.   I. Title.
BX4655.2.G48   1996
282'.092—dc20
    [B]
                                                                    96–24799
                                                                        CIP

This edition printed on acid-free paper and meets the American National Standards
Institute Z39.48 standard.

Interior design by Sherri L. Hoffman
Woodcuts by Paul B. Ritscher

Printed in the United States of America

---

96 97 98 99 00 01 02 03 /❖ QF/ 10 9 8 7 6 5 4 3 2

For Rosaleen A. Kirk

Contents

⟨∞⟩

Acknowledgments

⟨ɯɯ⟩

Thanks to my friends Donald E. Fishel and John B. Leidy, Jr., who are both amateur hagiographers and saint-watchers extraordinaire. They referred me to many miracle-working saints and guided me to books in which I could learn about them. Donald has a substantial library of biographies, which he generously let me raid.

I am also grateful to my friend and longtime editor, Ann Spangler, who gently compelled me to write a better book with her wise observations and suggestions. She made me work extra hard, probably because of her very high standards. But I suspect that she enjoyed putting it to me in return for my many practical jokes.

I tell you the truth, anyone who has faith in me will do what I have been doing. He will do even greater things than these, because I am going to the Father. And I will do whatever you ask in my name, so that the Son may bring glory to the Father.

—JOHN 14:12–13

Introduction:
Saints and Miracles

ᏋᎷᎯᎧ

We are all curious about miracles and are intrigued by those who seem capable of performing them. Wouldn't we love to experience a miracle of our own? An invasion of the supernatural would comfort us, assuring us that God cares enough to touch our lives.

Today, reports of miracles might raise an eyebrow or two, but few are shocked by claims of visions, healings, and other divine interventions. We live in an age that longs for the supernatural and that welcomes new evidence that there is more to life than what we can see and touch and feel.

The saints are men and women who can offer us the evidence we desire. They are wonder-workers who have fulfilled Jesus' prediction that his disciples would perform greater works than he did. The miracles of the saints are especially interesting because they are windows to the supernatural. But more than that, they show us what can happen when human beings are touched by the divine. Their lives paint a picture of what men and women can be like when they are transformed by God.

The saints have fascinated me for a long time. As a boy, I began reading books about them, and something about the extraordinary people I met in those biographies enchanted me. I was amazed by the way they lived and by the way many of them died.

The saints immediately joined the ranks of my childhood heroes, right up there with Superman and Batman, whose adventures I faithfully followed Saturdays at the movies. Gradually, I came to admire the saints even more than the superheroes. Superman, after all, was so far beyond anything I could ever aspire to. He was invincible and never got injured, but the saints, on the other hand, were mere humans. Sometimes they got hurt and did wrong or even evil things, and they were no strangers to failure. So the saints seemed to be a lot like me, and occasionally I thought that maybe someday I could be like them.

I was especially attracted to the martyrs. Their heroic sacrifices must have appealed to my youthful idealism. I remember reading that Saint Bartholomew, my namesake, had been "flayed alive." When I looked up "flay" in my dictionary, I was not even daunted to learn that it meant having one's skin torn off in strips. I think I even wished that someday I, too, could be a martyr. Subconsciously, I must have felt I was pretty safe. The newspapers were not reporting any martyrdoms in the south hills of Pittsburgh, where I lived.

As a boy, I might have agreed with Phyllis McGinley's daughter, who said, "It's easy to be a martyr. You only have to do it once." But the older I get, the more attached I have become to my body. Now the martyr's "doing it once" seems so fearsome as to be unimaginable. Once I told a friend that as a kid I might have prayed to be like the ancient martyrs who were stripped and left to freeze on an icy lake. "You think God heard your prayer," he said. "That's why you moved to Florida!" He was probably right.

Over the past several months I have spent every day with the saints. For the most part, I have enjoyed being with them. Now and then, however, their extremes have made me uncomfortable. Anthony's penances in the desert, for instance, are alien to me. I can't even tolerate sand between my toes when I'm sunning at the beach. The lifelong fasts of Vincent Ferrer and Francis of Paola are not for me. I am unable to go for many hours between meals without snacking. I was so distressed by the self-mutilations of Rose of Lima and Margaret of Cortona that I decided not to write about them. When Rose was praised for her lovely skin, she damaged it with lye. And out of a misguided sense of guilt over past sexual sins, Margaret carved scars in her beautiful face. In my view such actions have little to do with sanctity.

But I feel right at home when the saints let me see their humanity.

I won't soon forget how Teresa of Avila has delighted me. I will forever picture her scarfing down a partridge to the shock of a friend who thought she should be fasting. I will also remember her stifling a laugh in the back of a church as a priest denounced her from the pulpit. Francis of Assisi, who sometimes seems so otherworldly, has also endeared himself to me. On his deathbed he asked for marzipan, his favorite treat. He had just told one of his brothers to ask a longtime friend, a noblewoman of Rome, to bring him some, when she came to the door with a tray of the dessert. In a charming display of humanness, Francis bent the rule that forbade women to enter a friar's room. He instructed that the woman be called "brother," so she could approach his bed and serve him the marzipan.

As an inveterate practical joker myself, I cherish the high jinks of John Bosco. When two friends schemed to have him confined to an insane asylum, he had *them* locked up instead. I love the way Elizabeth of Hungary dealt with a fourteen-year-old boy. She confronted him about the way he dressed. Then, at his request, she prayed for him until he was almost overcome by God's presence. Now, where can I sign my teen up for that kind of treatment?

I have received great encouragement from Saint Patrick. When he was about fifty, he once offhandedly admitted that his youthful fervor was gone and he felt spiritually tepid. My own enthusiasm seems to have lost some of its zip, so Patrick's frankness gave me a boost.

One thing I've noticed is that the saints appeared to ignore the miracles that swarmed about them. Only a few seemed to deliberately work signs and wonders. These were the full-scale miracle workers like Francis of Paola, Vincent Ferrer, and John Bosco.

Some saints even seemed annoyed by their miracles. Lutgarde begged God to take back her gift of healing because long lines of petitioners kept her from prayer. Martin de Porres tried to hide his healing gifts by pretending to use herbs, compresses, and other medicines. Anthony of Egypt claimed to have no miraculous powers, but when he sent people away, their prayers were always answered. Francis of Assisi had to be persuaded to pray for the sick because he felt unworthy of any miracle. And the feisty teetotaler Catherine of Siena was once so embarrassed by the miraculous appearance of a medicinal wine in her behalf that she told Christ to undo the wonder. "Who asked you for this miracle, anyway?" she cried, with just a pinch of defiance.

Why are the saints' lives marked by so many miracles? Why did they experience so many visions, healings, and other supernatural events? I have some thoughts on that question.

The saints were lovers. With their whole heart and soul, they loved God, and they loved people with every ounce of their being. When they put their love in action, signs and wonders flowed. Out of pure affection, Theresa Margaret Redi sympathetically kissed an ailing friend, who was instantly healed by that little gesture. Anthony of Padua lovingly breathed a prayer over a troubled young man, who was mysteriously relieved and transformed on the spot. While in prison awaiting martyrdom, Perpetua and her companions were moved by love to pray for Felicity, who miraculously gave safe birth to her daughter one month prematurely.

Do I need to list more examples? I could go on for a long time. Scripture says that "God is love" and that "the love of God is shed abroad in our hearts." I believe that love causes, or at least occasions, miracles because God is in it.

If you look at it from another angle, you could say that the saints did not work any miracles at all. You could argue that not even those who produced the greatest miracles were actually wonder-workers. They just drew near and stayed close to Christ, who is the real Miracle Worker. The saints were intimate friends of Jesus, and their personal relationship with him was so secure that they could ask for favors and expect to receive them. Once, for example, Catherine of Siena teased Raymond of Capua by pretending that she couldn't obtain a healing for their friend who was deathly ill. When Raymond asked Catherine why she let the man lie dying, she said, "What? Do you think I am God that I can deliver someone from death?"

"Don't give me that!" said Raymond. "I know that Jesus does whatever you ask him to." Of course, Catherine had already asked, and Jesus had already healed their friend.

Many saints devoted themselves to Christ in his greatest miracle— the Cross. The mystery of Jesus' death and resurrection consumed Francis of Assisi, Teresa of Avila, and many others. When the saints invoked the power of the Cross, wonders occurred. Clare of Assisi once walked into an infirmary, called five times on the cross of Christ, and five sick sisters immediately got out of bed—healed. In the name of Christ crucified, Clare also stopped an army that was poised to attack her convent; Dominic restored to life a young man who had died in a fall from his horse; and Vincent Ferrer worked at least three thousand wonders. The saints' devotion to the cross of Christ overflowed in miracles.

Those are my thoughts on the subject. Let's see what you think after you read about the miracles of the saints.

Part One

Miracles of Love

The saints differ from us in their exuberance, the excess of our human talents. Moderation is not their secret. It is in the wildness of their dreams, the desperate vitality of their ambitions, that they stand apart from ordinary people of good will.

—PHYLLIS McGINLEY

God gave us saints, I am fond of saying, to show us that ordinary people can live extraordinary lives. He never meant for us to put them on pedestals or view them as superhumans far beyond anything we mortals could ever hope to be. The saints are not preternaturally gifted aliens from another planet, but human beings just like us. We esteem them, not because, like Superman, they have supernatural powers and can leap tall buildings in a single bound but because they show us how to live good lives—lives worth imitating.

When I look closely at the saints, I wonder if I grasp what it means to imitate them—really.

The saints did everything in extremes. No cost seemed too high. Me, I'm much more balanced. I count the cost all right, but I often find the price is steeper than I'm willing to pay.

Saint Theresa Margaret Redi was ill herself but put aside her own suffering to care for the sick sisters in her convent. I'm not that way. If I get sick, I hole up in bed and expect someone to wait on me.

Solanus Casey humbly accepted decisions of his superiors that severely restricted his life and ministry. For half a century he labored without complaint. I'm not like him. Even little inconveniences chafe me. I fight back, big time—just ask the clerks in our local stores.

What can I say about Saint Perpetua, who supervised her own martyrdom? Or Saint Martin de Porres? For fifty years he lived every moment of each day for God and for others.

When I stand myself beside these giants, I feel puny.

Comedian Stephen Wright says he once went to a convenience store that bragged it was "open twenty-four hours," only to find it closed. Later, the proprietor explained that his store *was* open twenty-four hours, just not twenty-four hours in a row! That's how I am in my imitation of the saints. I'm inconsistent. I try to be like the saints. But only in some ways. And not all of the time.

However, I keep looking at them. I try to stay close to them. I think that if I draw nearer to them, they might infect me with their virtue.

HEALING TOUCH

Saint Martin de Porres (1579–1639)

Virtue is our Everest, and those who climb highest
are most worth admiring.
—PHYLLIS MCGINLEY

Martin de Porres was a forerunner of twentieth-century social activists. Consider the remarkable record of his achievements, most of which he completed in addition to his routine tasks. Just reviewing his generosity may make us hyperventilate with exhaustion.

Martin single-handedly transformed his monastery into a service center, distributing food and clothing daily to hundreds of people. He also made it a prototype of a modern clinic, where the sick came to have their diseases cured. And they came in droves. Martin raised vast sums of money that he gave to the poor. Once he provided dowries for twenty-seven impoverished girls, who would have been unable to marry otherwise. He loved the homeless children of Lima, and for these waifs he planned, funded, and built an orphanage and school. He arranged for the best possible staff, sparing nothing to hire the most qualified caregivers and teachers.

He accomplished all this out of his own extreme poverty. His only possession was one shabby tunic, yet he was an inexhaustible source of comfort and help for thousands over a period of nearly fifty years. That, I think, is perhaps the real miracle in this saint's life.

Martin was born in Lima, Peru, on December 9, 1579. Less than fifty years before, Francis Pizarro and his conquistadors had seized the vast Peruvian empire of the Incas. In their rapacious pursuit of gold and power, the Spaniards cruelly destroyed the lives of the native people. Martin himself was a child of the conquest: He was the natural son of John de Porres, a conquistador, and Anna Velásquez, a free black woman. During the saint's lifetime, Peru was just beginning to recover from the Spanish invasions.

When Martin was twelve years old, he was apprenticed to a barber-surgeon, who trained him in the medical practices of the day. The youth became a medical expert, mastering the healing skills he would use life-long to serve others. At that time, Martin also apprenticed himself to Christ. The youthful disciple spent long periods in prayer every night. Often he was so rapt in contemplation that he seemed to lose contact with the world around him.

Martin used herbal medicines, poultices, and other natural remedies to heal the sick, but eventually he discovered he possessed supernatural gifts of knowledge and healing. Sometimes miracles happened directly through Martin's prayer or touch. The saint, however, worried that his supernatural gifts might draw undue attention to him and cause him to become proud, so he always tried to hide them by feigning to use some herb or other medicine.

Once the young saint visited a woman whom doctors had diagnosed with a life-threatening hemorrhage. The poor lady was so upset with anxiety that Martin had to repeatedly assure her she would not bleed to death. When he prayed for her, the Lord revealed to him that she would recover. Then, in a feeble effort to conceal his miraculous powers, he gave the sick woman an apple and told her to eat it. As he predicted, in a few days she had returned to perfect health.

In 1594, at age fifteen, Martin became a lay helper of the Friars Preachers at the monastery of the Holy Rosary in Lima. The Friars Preachers were the community of priests and religious brothers founded in the thirteenth century by Saint Dominic. Nine years later Martin entered the Dominican order by professing the vows of a religious brother.

Martin's healing gifts were so astonishing that it is tempting to want to recount the story of his life in great detail. But two miracles, in particular, reveal something of his remarkable character and gifts.

❦

Little did Francis Velasco suspect how difficult it would be to leave the monastery of the Holy Rosary once he had entered it as a novice.

Barely a month had passed when his father arrived to woo him away with the promise of riches and power. The senior Velasco was a man of considerable rank in Spain. In fact, the Spanish king had authorized him to pass on his prized post as secretary of the treasury to his son, Francis. This was an offer too alluring for the young man to resist. Afraid to face his superiors, Francis decided, instead, to steal away with his father at midnight. But just as he was about to slip off, he was startled by a surprise visitor. It seems that Martin de Porres was praying when suddenly he sensed the need to find Francis and confront him.

Never one to mince words, Martin accosted the young man. "Are you going to abandon the house of God for the office of the secretary of the treasury? It is better to serve God than to live in your father's house. Believe me, what you were unwilling to do out of love for God, you will do out of fear of God."

Martin's strange knowledge must have startled the youth, for he decided to remain in the monastery that night. A few hours later, Francis came down with a high fever. Once he had recovered, neither the midnight warning nor the illness were enough to convince him of his calling. He tried two more times to depart, each time becoming seriously ill.

The third and final time, Francis's illness was so severe that a physician by the name of Dr. Cisneto declared him a hopeless case. The doctor ordered him confined to his bed, where the fever soared and his pleural cavities swelled with fluid. There seemed little hope of his recovery. Then, one night, despite locked doors to both the building and the room, Martin de Porres stood beside the sick man's bed. In his hands he held an old brass brazier filled with live coals, a branch of rosemary, and a clean tunic. Martin dropped the rosemary on the coals, and the room filled with a blue, aromatic smoke. Then he helped Francis to his feet and wrapped him in a blanket.

The saint proceeded to turn the mattress, change the sheets, and sponge Francis's fevered body, finally covering it with the fresh tunic. Thus tenderly cared for, the youth stared at Martin and asked whether he would die.

"Do you want to die?" Martin replied.

"No."

"Then you will not die."

"But how did you enter the room when both doors were locked?"

"My boy," said Martin firmly, "who told you to meddle in such things?"

Then he departed—as swiftly and mysteriously as he had arrived.

Francis slept soundly. When he awakened in the morning, all of his symptoms were gone. In his amazement, Dr. Cisneto proclaimed it a miracle.

Martin made many such unexplained night visits to the sick, according to the testimony of his brothers at the monastery. He always seemed to arrive beyond locked doors, with an armload of healing paraphernalia.

On another occasion, Felician de Vega fell deathly ill while traveling through Lima. He was en route to take up his office as archbishop of Mexico. He suffered from fever and a severe, persistent pain on the side of his chest. All the doctors' remedies had failed to cure him. De Vega had heard about Martin's healing gifts, for despite all the pretenses he had used to disguise them, the saint had become famous. Desperate for relief, the archbishop demanded that Martin come immediately to his bedside.

Martin's superior ordered him to go in haste, so he had no time to gather his medicines. He worried that he had no decoys to distract attention from his miraculous powers, but he had no choice. He must obey. As soon as Martin arrived, the archbishop commanded him to stretch out his hand.

"But what would a prelate like Your Excellency want with the hand of a poor mulatto?" asked Martin, hesitantly. He knew what was coming.

"Didn't the Father Provincial tell you to do whatever I said?"

"Yes, my lord."

"Then put your hand here."

Marvelously, when Martin gently touched the archbishop's side, the pain seemed to evaporate.

Martin tried to pull back his hand. "Isn't that enough, my lord?"

"Leave it where it is," commanded the archbishop, and he pressed Martin's hand more tightly against his body. As he did, the fever and all discomfort vanished. Now altogether cured during this brief visit, De Vega unceremoniously sent Martin back to the monastery.

Embarrassed that he was compelled to display his gift, Martin returned to Holy Rosary determined to quell any temptation to pride. He grabbed a broom and began to sweep randomly and then found some toilets to clean.

"Brother Martin," asked one of the priests, "wouldn't you be better off in the palace of the archbishop of Mexico?"

Paraphrasing Psalm 84, Martin replied, "'I have chosen to be a slave in the house of my God.' Father, I think one moment spent in doing what I am doing right now is more important than many days spent in the house of the Lord Archbishop."

Martin did not spend much time thinking about miracles. They were God's business, not his. He spent his daylight hours indefatigably caring for others, especially Lima's poor. He devoted his nights to prayer and penance. He slept only sporadically and as little as possible, usually on a hard bench in the infirmary workroom.

Martin knew 1 Corinthians 13 by heart. "If I have a faith that can move mountains, but have not love, I am nothing. . . . It always protects, always trusts, always hopes, always perseveres." The profound charity described in that text shaped his life: He strove to make everyone around him comfortable but ignored his own discomfort. He fed the hungry poor, nourishing their bodies with food and their souls with good counsel.

Regularly Martin brought Lima's sick and infirm into the monastery to care for them, often in his own room. When some brothers complained, he found places for the sick at his sister's home nearby. He was frequently ill himself with a malarial fever, but he paid no attention to it.

Martin was in charge of the monastery's wardrobe. He kept the brothers properly dressed but also generously clothed the poor. The hungry always knew that Martin would feed them. At supper time he would scavenge the dining hall for food to serve the blacks, mulattos, Indians, and Spaniards who crowded outside the door. Often he gave away his own meals. At times when food was in short supply, it seemed to multiply as Martin dispensed it.

The thought of Martin de Porres makes me confront my own self-indulgence. My personal concerns seem to gobble up most of my money. Oh, I have had flashes of generosity in which I have mailed a check to a philanthropic organization. Rarely have I reached out personally to the poor. Now, I don't live lavishly, I tell myself, but I do see to it that I am well fed and comfortable. Perhaps imitating Martin de Porres, even in some small way, will chip away at my selfishness. It may take a miracle to move that mountain. But I will try.

☙❧

Love's Charter

If I speak in the tongues of men and of angels, but have not love, I am only a resounding gong or a clanging cymbal. If I have the gift of prophecy and can fathom all mysteries and all knowledge, and if I have a faith that can move mountains, but have not love, I am nothing. If I give all I possess to the poor and surrender my body to the flames, but have not love, I gain nothing.

Love is patient, love is kind. It does not envy, it does not boast, it is not proud. It is not rude, it is not self-seeking, it is not easily angered, it keeps no record of wrongs. Love does not delight in evil but rejoices with the truth. It always protects, always trusts, always hopes, always perseveres.

—1 Corinthians 13:1–7

LITTLE MIRACLES
OF AFFECTION
Saint Theresa Margaret (1747–1770)

ᏅᏋᎲᎧ

Be devoted to one another in brotherly love. Honor one another
above yourselves. Never be lacking in zeal, but keep your spiritual fervor,
serving the Lord. Be joyful in hope, patient in affliction, faithful in prayer.
—ROMANS 12:10–12

Anna Maria Redi was a lover. She made everyone around her feel valuable. If you had visited her, she would have made you the center of attention. She would have seen to it that you were comfortable, served you something to eat or drink, and then barraged you with questions about your life. "Now, tell me all about you," she would say. Anna Maria's smiling eyes would hold you fixed in her gaze, and she would celebrate everything you told her. You would have to tear yourself away from this charming young woman. And she would leave you with an exhilarating sense of approval.

Anna Maria showered this kind of affection on the nuns of Saint Teresa's convent in Florence, Italy, which she entered at age seventeen. As Sister Theresa Margaret, she regaled her sisters with personal kindnesses, which they enjoyed especially when they were sick. Her tender words and care touched all of them.

The elderly sisters of the cloister, in particular, were delighted with Theresa Margaret. She brought a gentle relief to their lives, which had been hardened by the rigors of the Carmelite rule. Her idealism stirred them to rekindle theirs, and they sensed in her a promise of refreshment.

Theresa Margaret's affection for her companions occasioned numerous little miracles. She was especially close to Mother Theresa Adelaide, an elderly woman who was stone deaf. Illness confined Theresa Adelaide to the infirmary, where the two friends, like a fading grandmother and a spritely granddaughter, were often absorbed in conversations. Those observing these remarkable visits were astounded because Theresa Adelaide could not hear a single word that others spoke, but she had no difficulty at all hearing Theresa Margaret.

The sisters also noticed another little miracle. When Theresa Adelaide lay dying, she would whisper Theresa Margaret's name. The young sister would come flying from far ends of the convent, where the sound of her friend's voice could not possibly have reached her.

Though Theresa Margaret was a stickler for the cloister's rule of life, on at least one occasion she put her love for a sister ahead of obedience to the letter of the law. And that charitable gesture occasioned a life-changing healing.

Sister Mary Victoria, one of the novices at Saint Teresa's, was tormented with a severe, chronic toothache. The affliction was so serious that the superiors wondered whether they should even accept her into the convent on a permanent basis. One day during a meal, Mary Victoria was quivering with pain. Moved by pity, Theresa Margaret leaned over and kissed her on the cheek. Immediately, she was free of the pain that plagued her. The toothache never recurred, and the young woman became a regular member of the community. The Carmelite rule forbade one sister to kiss another, but Theresa Margaret wasn't thinking about rules that day. She was thinking about love, and that led to a small gesture of kindness, and that led to a miracle.

Theresa Margaret died on March 7, 1770. For fifteen days her body lay exposed without any sign of decomposition. This miracle attracted thousands, who streamed to the convent from Florence and neighboring towns. One day the convent carpenter took a violet from the saint's bier and touched it to the face of a woman, who was then instantly healed of a disfiguring skin disease. Another workman took a flower and touched his son's arms. The boy was healed of a disease that had crippled him with inflamed joints. Theresa Margaret's affection seems to have lingered after her death. Her miracles ignited a spiritual renewal in the churches of Florence and in neighboring towns.

Mysteriously, Saint Theresa Margaret's body has remained physically incorrupt into the twentieth century, showing none of the usual signs of decay. You may wonder, as I do, why such things happen. When God allows something that seems to break the laws of nature, he must have a reason for it. Maybe he is telling us something. Something simple like, Look at this woman and love as she did. If you do, you may see miracles happen.

☙

Genuine Love

I desire to love you, O my God, with a love that is patient, with a love that abandons itself wholly to you, with a love that acts, and most important of all, with a love that perseveres.

Just as one who loves a creature thinks of it often, so let the lover of God have him often in his thoughts.

The mirror into which we must look in order to attain divine love is Jesus Christ.

If the actions of our neighbors had a hundred sides, we ought to look at them on the best side.

When an action is blameworthy, we should strive to see the good intentions back of it.

Let us do everything for love and, remembering that love longs for love alone, nothing can appear hard to us.

—SAINT THERESA MARGARET

bribe, two deacons bought some relief for Perpetua and her
[..]ey were temporarily transferred to a better part of the prison.
[..]s mother and brother brought her infant son to her there, and
[..] great comfort in nursing him again. "I spoke anxiously to my
[..] about my son," wrote Perpetua, "and encouraged my brother. I
[..]ded my son to their care. I was upset because I saw their con-
[..] me."

[..]mehow the resourceful Perpetua got permission to keep her baby
[..]er, which relieved her worry. "At once," she said, "I recovered my
[..]. My prison suddenly became my palace, and I would rather have
[..]there than anywhere else."

[..]uring this calm interlude, Perpetua received a vision that prepared
[..]o face her death courageously. In her mind's eye she saw a bronze
[..]er extending to heaven. It was narrow and its sides were lined with
[..]ks, knives, and other sharp tools. To make the climb, a person had to
[..]ceed with great care so as not to be shredded by the weapons. A huge
[..]rpent lurked at the base of the ladder, to terrify people and prevent
[..]em from ascending.

In the vision, Saturus, the instructor, climbed the ladder of martyrdom
[..]efore Perpetua. When he reached the top, he turned to encourage her
and warn her about the serpent. "In the name of Jesus Christ," she heard
herself declare, "he will not hurt me." Perpetua made the serpent's hea[..]
her first step, and it cowered under her foot. Then she climbed the l[..]
der unharmed. Thousands clad in white welcomed her into a beau[..]
garden. A tall man in shepherd's garb said, "Welcome, child," an[..]
her deliciously sweet milk curds to eat. When the vision ended, P[..]
felt strengthened in her resolve to die rather than to betray her [..]

In a few days the prisoners were taken to the public square [..]
The large crowd there snarled curses at them. First the judge i[..]

VISIONS

Saint Perpetua (181–203)

You must all stand fast in the faith and love one another.
And do not be weakened by what we have gone through.
—SAINT PERPETUA

Just before Perpetua was martyred, she wrote a touching account of
her last days. History has kindly preserved this remarkable personal
document for us, and, as I have read her words, I have become enchanted
with this wonderful woman. As she pours out her heart to me, I feel as
though I am visiting Perpetua in prison. But instead of my comforting
her, she is encouraging me. I would count myself fortunate to have been
one of her friends.

Maybe I feel close to Perpetua because I know several women who
are like her—an intriguing blend of seriousness and fun. No doubt you
know women like her: vivacious, eyes bright with affection, perhaps not
pretty but entirely lovely—these women stir admiration in everyone.

Women like Perpetua radiate inner strength. I call them "velvet
bricks" because they are both gentle and plucky. On the outside, tender,

accessible, and soft. On the inside, single-hearted, determined, and strong. Such women are competently in control of things. Awestruck, people stand back and let them have their way.

Perpetua lived in Carthage, North Africa, at the turn of the third century. She was a wealthy woman, the wife of a prominent man, and the mother of an infant son. Her mother and brother were probably Christians. Her father, a dyed-in-the-wool pagan, loved her as his favorite child.

At age twenty-two, Perpetua decided to become a Christian, and she and four friends received instructions in the faith from Saturus, their catechist. Her companions were Secundulus, Saturninus, and the slaves Revocatus and Felicity, who was in the last month of her pregnancy. In 203, just as they were preparing for baptism, Emperor Severus launched a general persecution. Anyone who refused to worship him as a god was threatened with capital punishment.

Apparently, because of their recent conversion to Christianity, Perpetua and the others were suspect. The local governor had them all arrested and confined to a private house while awaiting examination. Saturus, who was not with his five pupils when they were taken, would not let them face their trial alone. He marked himself for death by voluntarily joining them in their confinement.

The new Christians were all young, brimful with idealism, and strong of character, but they were not vaccinated against fear. Imagine the terrible thoughts that must have preyed upon Felicity. What would become of her unborn child? Would he survive her? Would her little innocent die a violent death with her? Perhaps she even doubted that she should stick by her choice to become a Christian. After all, what was a little incense offered to a conceited emperor if it spared her child? Whatever

tempting thoughts might have preyed o[...]
did not buckle.

Terrors must also have afflicted dough[...]
brave she was. The arrest had separated her[...]
she was still nursing. Her swollen breasts mus[...]
her of the pain she was about to cause her son. [...]
to hold and cuddle him again. Like Felicity, sh[...]
horrible fears about her baby's future. Would he b[...]
he someday hate her memory because she had aba[...]

The idea of Perpetua's death seemed to drive he[...]
made things a lot harder for her. Perpetua loved he[...]
sorrowed over his torment. One day he visited her[...]
change her mind about becoming a Christian.

"Father," she said, pointing to a water jug, "do you se[...]
Can it be called by any other name than what it is—a j[...]

"No," he replied.

"And just so, I cannot call myself by any other name[...]
am—a Christian."

At the word *Christian*, he quivered with rage and made [...]
ing gesture. Then he left his beloved daughter—defeated. A[...]
later, Perpetua and the others were baptized. After the cerem[...]
petua sensed God's inviting her to pray for physical stamina to[...]
ny torture that might precede her death.

Soon the six companions were confined in a hellish jail. "I wa[...]
[...]ied," said Perpetua, "because I had never experienced such darki[...]
[...]at a horrible day! Terrible heat because so many were cramm[...]
[...]ether! Rough treatment by the soldiers! To top it all, I was torment[...]
[...]nxiety for my baby."

With [...]
friends; th[...]
Perpetua[...]
she took[...]
mother [...]
comme[...]
cern fo[...]

So [...]
with h[...]
health[...]
been[...]

[...]
her [...]
lad[...]
ho[...]
pr[...]
se[...]
th[...]

Perpetua's companions, urging them to offer sacrifice. One by one, however, they confessed their faith and refused to comply. When Perpetua's turn came, her fear-crazed father rushed forward. He held her son before her and pleaded with her to reconsider.

"Spare your father," said the judge, "and spare your child. Offer sacrifice for the prosperity of the emperors."

"No," replied the saint.

"Are you a Christian?"

"Yes."

At this Perpetua's father tried to pull her away. The judge then had him beaten to stop his interference. Perpetua felt her father's pain as if she herself were struck, and she was overcome with grief for him. She was also obsessed with fear for her infant, but she still did not change her mind.

The judge ordered that Saturus, Saturninus, and Revocatus be scourged and Perpetua and Felicity be hit in the face. Then he sentenced them to a fight with wild beasts. Their executions would be the show at a military festival soon to be held in honor of the emperor's birthday. They were returned in chains to prison to await the event.

Because execution of pregnant women was not allowed, Felicity feared that she might suffer separately from her friends. However, Perpetua and the others prayed for her, and she immediately went into labor. It was a difficult, early delivery. One of the guards taunted Felicity, saying that the beasts would give her much greater pain. "What I am suffering now," she said, "I suffer by myself. But then another inside me will suffer for me, and I for him." She gave birth to a girl, whom Christian friends adopted and raised as their own daughter. About this time, Secundulus died in prison, spared of having to face the animals.

Just before the executions, the Roman tribune ruled that the prisoners could have no visitors. He feared that they might be magically spirited away. But plucky Perpetua confronted him. "Why can't you even allow us a little refreshment?" she asked. "Aren't we the emperor's own distinguished prisoners, since we're going to fight on his birthday? Wouldn't it be to your credit if we were to appear healthy before him at that time?" The saint's argument got to him, and, reddened with embarrassment, the official reversed his previous order. Friends and relatives would be allowed to visit.

The night before her death, Perpetua had another reassuring vision. She found herself in the amphitheater but was surprised to discover she was not facing wild animals. Instead, she was in a hand-to-hand contest with a malicious thug. She saw herself transformed into a mighty warrior ready for battle. Then an extraordinary man appeared, so tall that he towered above the arena. He had the appearance of an athletic trainer. He carried a rod and a branch full of golden apples, and he told her that her foe, if he won, would kill her with a sword. But if Perpetua defeated her foe, she would receive the bough.

When the two engaged in the fight, Perpetua instantly observed that her adversary was doomed. He was no match for her. She was then mysteriously lifted into the air, as though spiritual forces were assisting her. She thrust her enemy to the ground and crushed his head underfoot. The marvelous presider awarded her the bough, kissed her, and said, "Peace be with you, daughter." She walked triumphantly toward heaven's gate and the vision ended.

"Thus, I saw that I would not really be fighting with beasts," she said, "but with the devil. But I knew the victory to be mine." After recording this revelation, Perpetua wrote no more. An eyewitness recorded the rest of her story.

The next morning, the guards marched Perpetua and her companions to the arena, where they attempted to force the Christians to wear the robes of Roman priests and priestesses. Perpetua, however, resisted vigorously. "We agreed to pledge our lives," she said, "provided that we would not be made to do this." Because of her fearless intervention, they were allowed to enter the amphitheater dressed as they were. As they passed the crowds, Perpetua sang a psalm, and Revocatus, Saturninus, and Saturus shouted at the mob, warning them of God's judgment.

Saturninus and Revocatus were quickly dispatched, mauled to death by a leopard and a bear.

Then came Saturus with Pudens, the soldier in charge of the prisoners in jail. Because of their witness, he had become a Christian. Saturus was afraid of bears and had predicted he would be quickly killed by a leopard. Things happened just as Saturus had foretold. First, he faced a wild boar that did not harm him. However, it gored a soldier, who died within a few days. Saturus was then bound in stocks as bait for a bear, but the animal refused to leave his cage.

"It is exactly as I predicted," he told Pudens. "So now you may believe me with all your heart. I shall be finished off with one bite of a leopard." And then a leopard was loosed on him. It wounded him mortally, splashing him with blood. "Well washed!" roared the crowd. "Well baptized!" Covered with blood, Saturus said to Pudens, "Remember me, and remember the faith."

As for Perpetua, she never flinched. She seemed completely in control of herself. First, she and Felicity were tossed to the ground by a wild heifer, but Perpetua appeared hardly to notice. After the attack, she sat up and modestly pulled her ripped tunic over her thighs. Then she asked for a pin to fasten her hair in place so as not to appear to be in mourning. Assured that she looked dignified, she rose and helped Felicity to her feet. Together they were taken to one of the arena gates, where Perpetua exhorted her brother and some catechumens: "You must all stand fast in the faith and love one another. And do not be weakened by what we have gone through."

Finally, the soldiers killed the remaining companions by slitting their throats. Before their deaths, they greeted each other with a sign of peace. Perpetua shrieked as a nervous young soldier clumsily struck her with his sword. Then she did the unimaginable: She took his shaking hand and guided his weapon to her throat. "It was as though so great a woman," said an eyewitness, "could not be dispatched unless she herself were willing."

Saint Perpetua was a passionate lover of people. Her affection for family and friends caused her to be more concerned for them than she was for herself. She loved her father dearly, even though he felt she was treating him cruelly. And she loved her little son tenderly.

Above all, however, Perpetua was a passionate lover of God. Her love for him was a sun whose light subsumed all other loves. Her love for God intensified her love for family and friends. Had she put them ahead of him, I think she would have loved them less.

ᏇᎷᎮᏇ

The Saint's Paradox

Saints are paradoxical characters. They cheerfully endure themselves what they weep to see others endure.... They find riches in poverty, happiness in sorrow, and joy in pain. But the children of favor are fathered by a divine paradox: 'He who loses his life shall save it....' They take the paradoxical command literally. And logically enough, with the most paradoxical consequences.

—CLARE BOOTH LUCE

Miracles from Failures
Solanus Casey (1870–1957)

For whoever exalts himself will be humbled, and
whoever humbles himself will be exalted.
—Matthew 23:12

Solanus Casey may well be the most humble person you will meet in these pages.

Perhaps when you are dealing with saints, "humble" ceases to be a comparative adjective. When one always takes the lowest place, who can be lower? When one makes oneself the servant of all, who can compete? By definition, saints are superlatively humble.

The outline of Solanus Casey's life traces the pattern of biblical humility. From childhood to death, he lowered himself, serving everyone around him.

By human standards, he started his priestly service as a complete failure. He held the same menial job for forty years. He never owned anything. As far as the world was concerned, he was unimportant.

By spiritual standards, however, he was extremely successful. Tens of thousands benefited from his personal counsel and his miracles. Solanus Casey was one of the most prolific wonder-workers in Christian history. When he died in 1957, he was internationally famous. In one and a half days, twenty thousand people filed past his casket to say farewell to their beloved friend. All of them had been touched in some way by one of his miracles.

Solanus would have brushed off my high praise—if he even understood it. Every miracle amazed him. He saw each one as God's work, not his. He wept in awe with those who received miraculous healings. He never thought of himself as a miracle worker; he rarely thought of himself at all.

By age twenty-one, Casey was an accomplished, practical man. As a teenager, he had been one of the mainstays of his large midwestern family. He had already worked as a farmhand, lumberjack, brick maker, prison guard, motorman, and streetcar conductor. Then, in 1891, he witnessed a tragedy that set his life on a new course.

One cold, rainy afternoon as his streetcar rounded a curve in a rough part of town, it nearly hit a crowd of people gathered on the tracks. He brought it to a screeching halt, disembarked, and pushed through the crowd. But Casey was not prepared for the grisly scene he found there. A young, drunken sailor stood cursing over a young woman he had raped and stabbed repeatedly. The memory of this violent incident was seared in his brain. Casey began to pray daily for the girl and the sailor, and then felt he must also pray for the whole world. He gradually came to see this event as a type of the evil afflicting all human beings. From that time, young Casey searched his soul for a way he could be of greater service in the world. Finally, he decided he could best use his life to help others if he became a priest. That very year he entered the seminary of the diocese of Milwaukee, Wisconsin.

As a seminarian, Casey was only a mediocre student. Perhaps he struggled academically because the texts were in Latin but most of the instructors taught in German, and he had never mastered that language. For whatever reason, the seminary authorities told Casey in 1895 that he could not complete his studies there. They advised him to pursue his vocation as a laybrother in a religious order.

Frustrated but not defeated, Casey entered the Capuchin order in 1896. The Capuchins were a branch of the Friars Minor that Saint Francis founded in the thirteenth century. In 1897, he completed his novitiate at Saint Bonaventure Monastery in Detroit, Michigan, and spent the next seven years studying at the Capuchin seminary in Milwaukee. Again, his books were in Latin and his classes in German.

In 1902, failure threatened Solanus again because some of the seminary professors were opposed to his ordination. But Father Anthony, the elderly seminary director, championed him. "We shall ordain Father Solanus," he said, "and as a priest, he will be to the people something like the Curé of Ars." Saint John Vianney, the Curé of Ars, had been an extremely poor student but became a great confessor and wonder-worker. Little did the old priest realize how prophetic his words were.

When the time came for ordination in 1904, however, the seminary chose to limit Casey's priestly ministry. They decided he would be a "simplex priest." He could not administer the sacrament of penance or preach formally. Nor could he wear the hood from which the Capuchins took their name. These restrictions would have shattered others, but Solanus seems to have accepted them peacefully.

For the fifty-three years of his priestly ministry, Father Solanus Casey would never hear a confession, preach a mission, or conduct a retreat. He spent forty of those years as a porter—answering the door and greeting visitors to the monastery. That humble service provided the opportunity for his phenomenal career as a spiritual adviser and wonder-worker. Had he been given the full faculties of an ordinary priest, thousands might have been denied the graces of his friendship.

Father Solanus spent the first fifteen years of his priesthood quietly performing his duties at friaries in Yonkers and Manhattan, New York. He was transferred in 1921 to Our Lady of the Angels Friary, Harlem, New York, then mainly a middle-class white community. It was at Our Lady of the Angels that he first became known as a counselor and miracle worker. Visitors to the monastery soon discovered that the new porter was a patient listener who gave sound and inspiring counsel. Many would come just to speak with Father Solanus.

One of his assignments was the promotion of the Seraphic Mass Association. Capuchins used this association worldwide as a means of intercessory prayer. It was named in honor of Saint Francis of Assisi, who near the end of his life had a vision of a seraph, a six-winged member of heaven's highest order of angels. Capuchins everywhere prayed at their daily worship for those enrolled in the association. Shortly after Solanus started signing people up, extraordinary things began to happen. Reports of spiritual and physical healings streamed in. People were being healed of all sorts of ailments—pneumonia, heart disease, memory loss, insanity, lameness, cataracts, polio, alcoholism, gangrene, and blindness, to name just a few.

In November 1923 the Capuchin superior directed Solanus to keep a record of the miracles. Eight months later, the superior transferred Casey to Saint Bonaventure's in Detroit, his home base, where he could keep a close eye on the wonder-worker. In short order the new porter and his gifts attracted an ever-increasing following. Solanus began to lead a Wednesday afternoon healing service, and many people faithfully came to benefit from his prayers. For the next two decades, people from all over the world trekked to Saint Bonaventure's to receive the porter's ministry.

Thousands of miracles are briefly listed in Solanus's ledgers. We can consider only a few examples here.

ᏯᏫᏯᏯᎧ

William had long contemplated suicide. Solanus's notes do not give a reason for the despondency, but after much suffering, William concocted a careful plan for taking his life. He would book passage on a boat at Detroit for Cleveland and, as unobtrusively as possible, throw himself overboard along the way. His two sisters, who somehow got wind of his decision, kept him under close watch. Although riddled with fear for their brother, they didn't know what else to do.

During this critical time, William's father died, magnifying his distress and therefore his danger. At the funeral, however, one of his sisters happened to find a pamphlet that mentioned the work of Solanus Casey. That very day she visited the priest and asked his intercession for her troubled brother. Four short days later, the sister returned to tell Solanus that William had miraculously changed. Not only was he suddenly released from his despair, she reported, but he was "praying, and full of hope," and making plans to go back to work.

Immediately the sisters sought the priest's prayer for another brother, who had tuberculosis. Six months later, Solanus recorded in his ledger of miracles that the man had entirely recovered from the disease.

Raymond was an eight-month-old infant afflicted in both ears with a serious infection called mastoiditis. Before the days of sophisticated antibiotics, this disease was life threatening. One evening, when the baby's fever skyrocketed, he was hospitalized. The doctor planned to perform a dangerous surgery the next morning to save his life. He would drill holes in the bone behind each ear for drainage, the prescribed treatment for mastoiditis at the time.

The infant's mother was crazed with fear, and when hospital personnel were preoccupied, she smuggled Raymond from the building. Outside, she slipped into a waiting car, which her brother was driving, and they headed for home. Later, she told Solanus that she scarcely knew what she was doing at the time.

As they drove along the road, Raymond's mother suddenly recalled something about a priest at Saint Bonaventure's who could heal people. *Why had she not thought of it before?* "Drive to the monastery," she told her brother.

When they arrived, she carried Raymond straight to Solanus, who sat alone in his office near the door. The priest stood and extended his arms to receive the infant, while Raymond's mother told Solanus all that had happened—the disease, the planned surgery, the frantic escape. "O Father, help him," she sobbed.

Solanus handed Raymond back to his mother. He asked the child's name and entered it for intercessory prayer by the Seraphic Mass Association. Solanus then urged the mother to trust God and promised that he would not fail her. After that, he prayed over the infant.

"He will be better by morning," said Solanus, and at the door he assured her, almost casually, "And don't worry. He won't need an operation."

At home, she placed Raymond in his crib near her own bed. She touched his little face and could feel the raging fever; then, exhausted, she fell asleep for several hours. When she awakened, she picked up her baby and pressed him to her breast. Raymond was cold and motionless. For a moment she feared that he had died. But then she felt him breathing and realized that he was in a deep sleep. Miraculously, Raymond seemed to be out of danger.

She and her husband whispered a prayer of thanks and then headed to tell Solanus the good news of Raymond's sudden recovery. The priest showed no surprise. When the couple tried to thank him, he told them to express their gratitude to God. The next day, the doctors examined Raymond and declared that no operation was necessary, inasmuch as he had returned to normal health.

Luke was a businessman-turned-alcoholic who lived in a flophouse. Once, he tried, cold turkey, to quit drinking, and he roamed the streets of Detroit, hoping to get better. He eventually wandered to the monastery, where he poured his heart out to Father Solanus.

"When did you get over your sickness?" asked the priest finally.

"You mean my drunk, Father?" asked Luke.

Solanus laughed. Luke described it as a "gentle, encouraging kind of laugh."

"I went out from that talk," said Luke, "strengthened and with a free, elevated spirit. I never again took an alcoholic drink."

So they came to Saint Bonaventure's every day. By the hundreds, suffering people came to transfer their burdens to the stout spiritual shoulders of this saintly priest. Some sought life direction. Many wanted relief from problems—failures at work, disloyalty of friends, or relatives. Others needed help pacifying family squabbles. Many came seeking healing for themselves or loved ones. Solanus always responded with gentle, commonsensical advice and a compassionate warmth that soothed petitioners. He would then enroll them in the Seraphic Mass Association for intercession, pray for them, exhort them to trust God, and send them off with a word of encouragement.

It is hardly surprising that Solanus Casey paid an enormous personal price in his service. He typically worked eighteen-hour days, praying during the time he was not counseling guests. At night, in the chapel, he was often found sound asleep before the altar. Once a brother observed that he chose a rather hard bed. "Don't worry about me," said Solanus, "I'm sleeping on the soft side of the planks."

He occasionally found the daily litany of people's suffering difficult to bear. "Sometimes," he wrote, "it becomes monotonous and extremely boring, till one is nearly collapsing; but in such cases, it helps to remember that even when Jesus was about to fall the third time he patiently consoled the womenfolk and children of his persecutors, making no exceptions. How can we ever be as grateful as we ought to be for such a vocation—for such privileged positions. . . ."

And how can we be grateful enough for saints like Solanus Casey?

You may wonder why Solanus has no "Saint" before his name. That is because the Roman Catholic Church has yet to complete the process of formally recognizing him as a saint. But he is well underway to receiving that recognition. Even if he were never to be acknowledged thus, however, I would always think of him as Saint Solanus Casey.

ᘓᗯᗽᕒ

Reflections of God

If the moon is beautiful as it reflects the light of the sun at so great a distance, what will be the beauty of the saints who for all eternity and not at a distance, will reflect the divine image of God?

—SOLANUS CASEY

Part Two

ᘒᙏᙏᓚᓂ

Mystics
and
Miracles

Blessed are the pure in heart,
for they will see God.

—MATTHEW 5:8

Love is as strong as death,
its jealousy unyielding as the grave.
It burns like blazing fire,
like a mighty flame.
Many waters cannot quench love;
rivers cannot wash it away.

—SONG OF SONGS 8:6–7

Contemporary believers are diligent in their search for the supernatural. Many appear to be on endless journeys, seeking God everywhere. "People behave as though God were lost," says theologian Augustine DiNoia, "and we must send out search parties to find him." We feel that God is distant, even aloof. We believe that we must pursue him aggressively if we are to touch him and he is to touch us.

Do you think that's the way it really is? Are we the hunters and God the prize? Or is it just the opposite—God hounds us until we let ourselves be found?

That's the way it was with the saints. Take Saint Lutgarde, for example. This effervescent and beautiful young woman was surrounded by friends. She gave little thought to God. Until he caught up to her.

Anthony of Egypt is also a case in point. He was a young landowner of twenty before God took hold of him and transformed him into one of history's most passionate and colorful saints.

Lutgarde and Anthony were pearls of great price, and God was the gem merchant who desired them above all. Isn't that the way it is with us? Don't we sometimes run—even covering our tracks as we go—until God finds us? I love knowing that God values me enough to pursue me. It does wonders for my self-image—if I can only slow down long enough to let him overtake me.

Lutgarde and Anthony were mystics. So were Catherine of Siena, Elizabeth of Hungary, and Clare of Assisi. We get the word *mystic* from a Greek root that means "mystery." A mystic is a person who is "introduced into the mysteries." Broadly speaking, all Christians are mystics. We believe that by faith we are initiated into the mysteries of Christ's death and resurrection. But most Christians are not mystics in the way that Saint Catherine was because they have yet to penetrate the Christian mysteries in depth. That's what sets a true mystic apart from the crowd.

Mystics enjoy a special closeness to the supernatural. They get rid of all the clutter in their hearts to make more room for the divine. Often they practice severe self-discipline so they can replace their fleshly desires with longings for God alone.

Mystics frequently experience miraculous phenomena and exercise extraordinary powers. They may seem to lapse freely into ecstasy and have been observed at prayer to be out like lights, sometimes for hours. Catherine went limp in ecstasy. Lutgarde was seen "floating" off the ground. Martin de Porres was said to have passed through locked doors to serve the sick. Anthony of Egypt seemed to glow with preternatural radiance. What explains such things?

The mystics' union with God can give us a clue to understanding the unusual supernatural manifestations in their lives. They are granted a foretaste of heaven, and the supernatural thoroughly penetrates their earthly lives. For brief periods their humanity appears to take on divine qualities. God, of course, is behind it all. Saint Catherine liked to say that "All the way to heaven is heaven because Christ said 'I am the way.'" Heaven has come down to earth. Supernatural reality is so present in some people that it cannot be contained in mere earthen vessels. It breaks out in ecstasies and other miraculous phenomena.

You might think that mystics are so absorbed with God that they can do nothing but worship him. The mystics of old did pray for long stretches, but they were also activists. Saints like Catherine, Martin de Porres, and Elizabeth exhausted themselves in service all day long. Then they would pray most of the night. So as not to disturb her sleeping husband, Elizabeth asked her maid to quietly awaken her for night vigils. Anthony prayed all the time, yet he was very busy. His community-building activity in the desert preserved the Christian ideal for the church of his time, and we still feel the influence of his achievements.

Which do you think came first—the saints' prayer or their action? Did contemplation of God move them to express their love for people? It may have been so with Lutgarde and Anthony. Or did the saints' efforts to love people, who were sometimes not easy to love, drive them to prayer? That may have been so for Catherine and Elizabeth. Perhaps both impulses were working at different times in all of them.

Do you think that if we imitated both their prayer and their action, God might catch up to us? Do you think we might even experience a miracle? Since it's up to God anyway, it's certainly worth a try.

⟨∞⟩

Miracles That Made Peace

Saint Catherine of Siena (1347—1380)

⟨⟩

By this all men will know that you are my disciples,
if you love one another.
—JOHN 13:35

Catherine of Siena was an international political figure and one of the most celebrated women in history. To some she is a feminist hero, one of only two women named as a "doctor of the church." (The other is Saint Teresa of Avila.) We think of her as an Eleanor Roosevelt with a halo. We envision her dressed in the fourteenth-century equivalent of a tailored suit, traversing Europe to tell popes and emperors how to run their empires.

There's a germ of truth in that portrayal of Catherine. But only a germ. Catherine worked mightily to reconcile warring popes and emperors. She did most of that work, however, through letters and on her knees.

To get a more accurate view of Catherine, imagine a scruffy, not-so-respectable version of Mother Teresa. Catherine was not a nun, however, but a member of the Dominican Third Order. Thus she was committed to follow the life pattern of the Friars Preachers as a layperson. Think of her as an old-fashioned Italian matriarch, pious but sharp-tongued, who scandalized as many people as she influenced. Picture this short, frail lady, garbed in worn, rough clothes, in some of her typical daily activities:

Saint Catherine managed a large household of followers, all of whom called her "Mama." She and her disciples lived in poverty. They begged for everything they needed.

She fasted severely but always saw that her friends were well fed. She cooked food and baked bread. Sometimes she prayed for a miraculous multiplication or delivery of food.

Catherine prayed many hours at a time. She seemed to become weightless when she was deep in prayer. People claim to have seen her floating a few inches off the ground.

Catherine read the thoughts and knew the temptations of her associates, even at long distances. She saw people's secret sins and confronted such persons, urging them to repent. So effective was she that the Friars Preachers had to designate three priests to handle the confessions of her penitents.

She interceded fiercely for hardened criminals in Siena's jails. Even blasphemous prisoners embraced the Gospel when she visited them.

She cared for the sick. Plague victims were miraculously healed when she prayed or touched them.

Finally, Saint Catherine did offer advice to popes and princes. However, she was not so much an international politician as she was a spiritual director, and her venue was not the entire world but a small quadrant in northern Italy. The issue that concerned her most was not governmental but ecclesiastical. Catherine's passion was for the unity of the church.

In 1376, Catherine labored to repair a breach between Pope Gregory XI and a league of north Italian cities led by Florence. Since 1305, the papacy had become a cause of contention between the French and the Italians. Turmoil in Rome and conflict with the emperor had forced the popes to retreat to Avignon in southern France. Catherine shared the popular Italian desire to restore the papacy to Rome. Pope Gregory XI was willing to make the move, but his powerful French advisers resisted.

Catherine conducted a campaign of letters to all sides and offered to mediate directly. She wrote Pope Gregory XI six times, exhorting him to return to Rome. The pope said that Catherine's tone was "intolerably dictatorial, a little sweetened with expressions of her perfect Christian deference." Encouraged by the Florentines, she went to Avignon on a peacemaking mission.

Apparently the pope had made a secret vow to move back to Rome, and this vow was revealed to Catherine. When she met the pope at Avignon, she didn't hesitate to use that inspired bit of information to pressure him. "Keep the promise you have made," she urged, to his great surprise. Not long after this encounter, Gregory XI returned the papacy to Rome. Catherine's efforts to reconcile the pope and the Italian cities finally succeeded during the reign of Urban VI, Gregory's successor.

More than anything, Catherine was consumed with a passion for God and for the welfare of others. And as she pursued those passions, miracles happened.

Once Catherine prayed for two condemned prisoners, who were then profoundly touched by the supernatural. Here's how it happened: Two of Siena's hardened criminals had been sentenced to a brutal public death.

They were driven about town in a cart while executioners tore at their bodies with red hot pincers. The malefactors showed no trace of remorse for their crimes and roared curses and blasphemies at the people who lined the streets. They had refused to speak with the priests who had offered to prepare them for death.

Providentially for the prisoners, Catherine happened to be visiting a friend that day who lived on one of the roads the cart had chosen. "Mama, look at this horrible sight," said the woman as the tumultuous parade went by. While the saint stood in the window observing the terrible scene, she was moved by compassion. In her mind's eye, she saw a mob of demons ready to punish the condemned men even more sadistically in hell.

Immediately she began to pray for the two unfortunates. "My most merciful Lord," she said with her characteristic frankness, "why do you show such contempt for your own creatures? Why are you letting them suffer such torture now? And even more vicious torture by these hellish spirits?" Catherine never beat around the bush, even in conversations with God.

Shortly thereafter, to the amazement of all, both criminals stopped shouting curses and cried out for a priest. They wept and confessed their sins to him. The crucified Christ, they claimed, had appeared to them urging repentance and offering forgiveness. They told the crowd that they expected to be with Christ in heaven, and then they submitted peacefully to their execution. The whole town was mystified by this miraculous turn of events, but Catherine's close friends knew that she had had something to do with it. For many days after the dramatic conversions, the saint was heard to say, "Thanks, Lord, for saving them from a second prison."

Saint Raymond of Capua, Catherine's spiritual director and biographer, assisted her in another notable conversion. Living in Siena was a celebrated rascal named Nanni di Ser Vanni, who specialized in stirring up private feuds. His schemes often led to violent outbursts, and once someone was even murdered as one of these schemes unfolded. No one could pin any charges on Nanni, but the whole town was wary of him. Raymond said that he was so slippery that he would trick God if he could.

Catherine wanted a chance to persuade Nanni to change his ways, but he avoided her, said Raymond, as "the snake avoids the charmer." One of her disciples, however, convinced Nanni to visit her and to listen to what she had to say. Nanni thought he would hear the saint out and then go about his business. He had no idea what he was in for.

Raymond was present when Nanni met Catherine. She greeted him politely, offered him a seat, and asked why he had come.

"I came," he said, "because I promised a mutual friend that I would. He asked me to tell you the truth about my affairs, and I will. But don't imagine that you can make me stop."

Then Nanni candidly admitted that he was behind several murderous plots presently seething in Siena. In her typical blend of sweetness and sharpness, Catherine warned him that his soul was in mortal danger, but Nanni adamantly refused to change his behavior.

When Catherine realized that he had turned a deaf ear, she began to pray quietly and then immediately drifted into an ecstasy. Raymond covered for her and picked up the conversation. Shortly, Nanni found himself talking about his machinations. He was behind at least four feuds that were rocking Siena. He described one in detail and expressed his willingness to let Raymond quell that disturbance.

Then an extraordinary thing happened. Nanni made a move to leave but was overwhelmed by remorse. "My God," he said, "how contented I feel in my soul from having said I shall make peace! Lord God, what is this power that draws me? I can't go and I can't say no." After that, he promised to do anything Catherine directed to set things right.

Catherine awakened and said, "I spoke to you, and you would not listen, so I spoke to God and *he* got your attention." Then she gently urged Nanni to make peace with God, which he did, on the spot. Over the next few weeks she helped him reconcile with all his enemies, and from that time on Nanni lived an upright life. The scoundrel had experienced a complete personal transformation. Later on, to express his gratitude, he deeded to Catherine a castle near Siena, which she turned into a convent.

When the plague struck Siena, Catherine and her friends courageously tended the sick. The disease eventually struck Matteo, the rector of the city's hospital and a close friend of Catherine. When she got the news, she hurried off to see him. She was hot with anger at the plague, and even before the saint reached his bed she began shouting from a distance: "Get up, Matteo, get up! This is no time for lying in a soft bed!" At this command, all Matteo's fever, swelling, and pain disappeared.

Catherine slipped away to avoid attracting attention. Just then Raymond—unaware of the miracle—approached and begged her to pray for Matteo's recovery.

"What?" exclaimed Catherine, pretending to be offended. "Do you think I am God that I can deliver someone from death?"

"Don't give me that!" said Raymond. "I know that Jesus does whatever you ask him to."

Catherine smiled mischievously. "Cheer up. He won't die this time."

A short time later, Raymond shared a hearty celebration meal with Matteo, who a few hours before could barely open his mouth.

One day, in Catherine's neighborhood, a balcony collapsed, hurtling a woman to the ground. The victim lived near Catherine, and they had become friends. The woman was so badly cut and bruised by falling debris that she could not move. Catherine visited her injured friend and tried to comfort her. In a soothing gesture, she touched the woman, and the pain immediately left that spot. The woman begged Catherine to touch another place that hurt. There, too, the pain vanished. So they kept it up—the woman requesting that Catherine touch injured places until all the pain was gone. The woman had recovered completely. "Catherine," she told everyone, "has cured me by touching me."

Once, on a visit to Pisa, Catherine found herself in a seriously weakened condition. Raymond of Capua and other friends sought a remedy to strengthen her. They searched for some vernaccia, a wine with healing properties. Vernaccia was supposed to bring relief when applied to a sick person's temples and wrists. They asked a neighbor, who always stocked vernaccia, to give them a decanter. "I would gladly give you a barrel if I had it," he said, "but it has been empty for three months." For emphasis, he pulled the spigot from the barrel, then stared in amazement as wine gushed forth. So, Catherine's friends miraculously obtained medicine for her.

To the saint's great embarrassment, news of the miracle spread throughout Pisa. Catherine was up and about in a few days, and people were excited to see her. "Who is this," someone teased, "who doesn't drink wine but can fill an empty cask with it?"

Catherine was displeased with the hubbub. "O Lord," she prayed with near-irreverent familiarity, "why have you willed to inflict me with the pain of this mockery? Who asked you for the wine, anyway? For a long time I've deprived my body of wine, but now wine is making a joke of me. By your infinite mercy, have pity on me! Dry all the wine up and put an end to this chatter."

The wine turned as sour as vinegar and was no longer potable. The owner of the miracle barrel and those who came to sample the wine stopped talking about it. Catherine was delighted.

In 1378, Christendom was torn by the Great Western Schism. This time, two men claimed to be the pope, one based at Avignon and another at Rome. Catherine spent herself in prayer and advocacy on behalf of Urban VI, who called her to advise him in Rome. Her intensive efforts to win support for him wore heavily on her. In 1380, Catherine had a vision in which the church, depicted as a great ship, seemed to crush her. Her response to this vision was to pray and offer her suffering on behalf of the church. A few months later, in April, she died of a paralytic stroke.

I liked Catherine of Siena when I knew her superficially as an ambassador who straightened out affairs of church and state. I admire her more now that I have become better acquainted with her. She was a sweet curmudgeon, like several of my Italian aunts. The beatitude says, "Blessed are the peacemakers for they shall be called children of God." That text sums up Catherine's life perfectly.

∞

Unselfish Love

I have placed you in the midst of your fellows that you may do to them what you cannot do to me, that is to say that you may love your neighbor freely without expecting any return from him, and what you do to him I count as done to me.

—FROM THE DIALOGUE OF SAINT CATHERINE OF SIENA

THE "ACCIDENTAL" MYSTIC
Saint Lutgarde of Aywières (1182—1246)

ᏀᎷᎯᎧ

The charm of Saint Lutgarde is heightened by a certain earthly simplicity. Lutgarde for all her ardent and ethereal mysticism, remained always a living human being of flesh and bone.
—THOMAS MERTON

Lutgarde became a saint by "accident." Her father squandered her dowry in a bad business deal, and her wealthy mother financed her entry into a convent. In 1194, at age twelve, Lutgarde went to live at the Benedictine monastery of Saint Catherine, which was near Saint-Trond, close to Liége and the Meuse River.

At first, Lutgarde was simply a boarder at Saint Catherine's, coming and going as she pleased. She even entertained young men as guests. In her mind these were innocent friendships, and she seemed flattered by the attention. One young fellow, however, fell in love with her. He even tried to persuade her to run off with him.

One day as this admirer whispered sweet nothings to Lutgarde, Christ himself intervened. He appeared to her in a blazing vision and showed her the wound in his side. "Stop seeking the pleasure of this unbecoming affection," he said. "See here, forever, what you should love, and how you should love."

Lutgarde was stunned and terrified and abruptly dismissed her astonished suitor. "Get away from me, you bait of death," she said, "I belong to another Lover." In that moment the course of her life was set. She began to pray more seriously and do penance more rigorously. The nuns at Saint Catherine's observed Lutgarde's conversion icily, doubting that this worldly girl would have much stick-to-itiveness.

The sisters soon had to admit they were wrong. Not only did Lutgarde persevere in prayer, but she also learned to speak with Christ quite familiarly. When the nuns interrupted her with tasks, she would say, "Wait here, Lord Jesus. I'll come right back as soon as I'm finished." The sisters' skepticism melted when they observed Lutgarde's personal worship. At such times, they felt their hearts mysteriously warmed by the radiance that seemed to flow from her.

Lutgarde seemed unimpressed with her divine favors. She had received, for example, a gift of healing. When word about it spread, hosts of petitioners came to her for healing of minor illnesses. Lutgarde became increasingly annoyed with these requests because they interrupted her prayer. "Why did you go and give me such a grace, Lord?" she asked. "Take it away, please!" Then she impishly added, "But give me something better!"

As an alternative, the saint requested a miraculous understanding of Latin. Throughout the day the sisters used that language in choir for chanting psalms and prayers. Lutgarde prayed fervently but did not grasp a word of what she was saying, so she thought that a greater understanding of the texts would magnify her devotion. The grace was granted, and Lutgarde was able to understand the Latin words. But to her disappointment, this enlightenment did not enhance her worship, as the light did not seem to get from her head to her heart.

Lutgarde again complained to the Lord. Her new intellectual gift, she said, depleted her prayer instead of strengthening it. "What, then, do you want?" the Lord seemed to say.

"Lord," she said, "I want your heart." She thought she heard Jesus reply, "But Lutgarde, I want *your* heart."

"Take my heart," Lutgarde prayed in response. "May your heart's love be so mingled and united with my heart that I may possess my heart in you. May it ever remain there safe in your protection." In Lutgarde's first vision, Christ had shown her his heart. Now it seemed to the saint that he linked his heart so closely with hers that she shared his core desires. From then on Lutgarde felt that she participated in Christ's deepest longing—his desire to redeem sinful human beings. This passionate, Christ-inspired charity shaped the rest of her life.

Lutgarde's ascent to mystical heights did not go to her head. She never became arrogant or otherworldly. Her simplicity, friendliness, and generosity authenticated her spirituality and won the trust and affection of her sisters. In 1205, these nuns, who had once thought Lutgarde would never make it, named her prioress of Saint Catherine's.

This election horrified Lutgarde because her new duties took her away from prayer. It prompted her to seek a place in another monastery. In 1206, she moved to Aywières, a Cistercian house secluded in a lovely valley near Brussels. Aywières appealed to Lutgarde because it was both austere and exclusively French speaking. There she could practice her spiritual disciplines with no danger of being drafted for community office. Lutgarde was happy that she spoke only Flemish. She was not about to pray for the grace to understand French!

For the next forty years Lutgarde labored in prayer and penance to support Christ's purposes. She saw herself as a partner with Christ in his work. Three times at Aywières the saint undertook seven-year fasts in reparation for others' sins. The first time, she subsisted on bread and liquids as she prayed for the Cathars—these heretics held that the material world was evil and denied that Jesus was a human being. Lutgarde believed that Christ commissioned her second seven-year fast as an offering for sinners at large.

Near the end of her life Lutgarde went on a third seven-year fast, during which she prayed for protection of the church from Emperor Frederick II's efforts to destroy it. She prophesied that "this man who secretly desires the overthrow of the church is either going to be humbled by the prayers of the faithful, or else he will soon depart this life and leave the Church in peace." Both prophecies were fulfilled a few years after the saint's death: Frederick II was first deposed, and then he died suddenly in 1250.

Saint Lutgarde's graceful tenderness charmed the sisters at Aywières. She always had kind words for the troubled and sensible advice for the perplexed. The nuns loved her for it. She never forgot others' needs, even when she was at prayer.

Once, after receiving Communion, the saint was enjoying a pleasant reverie in Christ's presence. But it was supper time and she was hungry. Nearby in the infirmary was her friend Sister Elizabeth, who was very ill. Her affliction had so weakened her that she was bedridden and had to be fed at frequent intervals, day and night. The spunky Lutgarde then prayed, "Lord, this is not the right time for me to have all this delight and sweetness. Why don't you go to Elizabeth . . . and take possession of her heart? Let me go get something to eat and build up my strength." So Lutgarde went off to eat, and Elizabeth was suddenly strengthened. She not only did

came a hermit. Later on, he would pursue a solitary life in the
an desert.

he young monk learned the ascetical life from other recluses who
nearby on the outskirts of the city. Imitating their Christian behav-
e diligently applied their teachings on prayer and other spiritual prac-
When he noticed a virtue in one of them, he worked at acquiring it.
ursued it doggedly until he had mastered the quality even more per-
y than his model. Saint Athanasius, Anthony's biographer, said that
was a perfect handicraftsman in matters that related to fear of God."

Anthony developed a pattern that he followed for eighty-five years.
ate once a day, never before sunset, and his meal consisted of six
nces of bread soaked in water, sometimes seasoned with a little salt.
hen he was elderly, he occasionally allowed himself a few palm dates
d a little oil. He wore sheepskin garments with the hair against his
ody. Weaving mats of palm fronds was his ordinary work. Later, when
e moved to the desert, he tilled a small garden, growing wheat to make
his bread and vegetables for his guests.

All day and all night, Anthony prayed. At any time, a visitor might
find him rapt in mystical ecstasies. He loved to pray at night and sometimes complained that the sunrise robbed him of the greater light of inner
contemplation.

Once, however, he became depressed because he did not feel strong
enough for lengthy prayer. He took comfort from a vision in which an
angel showed him the value of balancing prayer and work. The angel
alternately wove mats and then rose to pray. After a while, the angel said,
"Do this, and you will find relief." So the saint adjusted his pattern. However, Saint Athanasius says, he continued to pray a little while he worked.

Anthony's monastic career progressed through three stages. For fifteen years he lived in huts and tombs near the village of Koman. Then,

not *need* any food, but she could not even eat for some time. Soon she
was completely well and returned to live the full community life.

On another occasion, Lutgarde came late to choir. She found Sister
Matilda, who was deaf, weeping because she could not hear the beautiful singing. Overcome with compassion for her friend, Lutgarde knelt
and prayed briefly. Then she wet her fingers with spittle and put them in
Matilda's ears. Matilda felt something snap, and her ears roared with the
mellifluous voices of sopranos chanting the psalms. Paradoxically, Lutgarde did not seek healing for herself. Eleven years before her death in
1246, she lost her sight. She cherished the blindness as a blessing that
removed her from distracting worldly involvements.

I first heard of Saint Lutgarde of Aywières when I discovered Thomas
Merton's biography of the saint in a friend's library. I'm glad I met this
lovely woman. Her tenacious idealism, rigorous asceticism, and fervent
mysticism intimidate me, I confess. But I revere her for them. And I, like
Thomas Merton and the sisters at Aywières, am charmed by her friendly,
affectionate attention to others.

⊙⟶⟶⟵⊙

A Tiger Lily of a Saint

In the month of June, when the sun burns high in the bright firmament and when Cistercian monks, like all other farmers, hitch
up their teams and go out to gather in the wheat, Saint Lutgarde's
Day comes around. She is a saint whose spirit is as ardent and colorful as the June weather and as bright as the tiger lilies that enliven
the fields and roadsides in the month in which we celebrate her
memory.

—Thomas Merton

MIRACLES IN THE DESERT

Saint Anthony of Egypt (251–356)

꩜

Anthony was like a good physician given to the people of Egypt. For whoever came to him afflicted who did not go away rejoicing? Whoever came to him full of rage who was not enriched with graciousness and long-suffering? And what person ever came to him troubled in mind who did not go away with it composed? . . . People loved him so much that after he had departed from this world, his memory never died. Everyone took courage from the repetition of his triumphs and of his words.

—SAINT ATHANASIUS

Saint Anthony was not the first ascetic, but he was the first monk who fled the city to pursue God in the desert. Or perhaps to let God find and catch him there.

"Ascetic" comes from a Greek word for "athlete." Christian ascetics were spiritual athletes, and the Gospels were their workout programs. Prayer, fasting, and charitable works were their exercises. Jesus and Paul were their trainers. The Holy Spirit, as they often said, was their strength, while God was their prize, and they were his.

47

...as born near Memphis in Egypt... ...disengaged from ordinary life to ... ...God. Men and women alike had become ...called "monks," taking their name from a Greek ... the women were "nuns," "nonnae" in Latin, mea... worldly desires. Some ascetics sought their solitude... of the towns. For safety's sake, the nuns stayed wi... resided together in households, but the monks lived... skirts of cities in huts, caves, or abandoned tombs.

These ascetics pursued virtue by avoiding secular so... taining contact with their local Christian communitie... had a lot to flee. The Roman Empire was lustful, viole... and its culture made evil attractive. Monks and nuns ab... persuasively wicked environments because they believed th... helped them conquer their own evil tendencies.

Anthony was twenty when his parents died and left him... for his little sister. A few months later, at church one Sunda... from the Gospels changed his life. "If you want to be perfect," ... the lector, "go, sell your possessions and give to the poor, and... have treasure in heaven. Then come, follow me" (Matthew... Anthony was certain God had spoken right to him. He respon... selling his parents' estate and the possessions he had inherited. ... tributed the proceeds to the poor, reserving only enough to provi... his sister's future.

A short time later, Anthony heard another Sunday gospel dec... "Do not worry about tomorrow" (Matthew 6:34). Again, he took ... words personally and gave as alms the money he had set aside for his s... ter. He found the little girl a home with a household of nuns, the fir... convent in recorded history. Then he moved to a hut on the edge of town...

not *need* any food, but she could not even eat for some time. Soon she was completely well and returned to live the full community life.

On another occasion, Lutgarde came late to choir. She found Sister Matilda, who was deaf, weeping because she could not hear the beautiful singing. Overcome with compassion for her friend, Lutgarde knelt and prayed briefly. Then she wet her fingers with spittle and put them in Matilda's ears. Matilda felt something snap, and her ears roared with the mellifluous voices of sopranos chanting the psalms. Paradoxically, Lutgarde did not seek healing for herself. Eleven years before her death in 1246, she lost her sight. She cherished the blindness as a blessing that removed her from distracting worldly involvements.

I first heard of Saint Lutgarde of Aywières when I discovered Thomas Merton's biography of the saint in a friend's library. I'm glad I met this lovely woman. Her tenacious idealism, rigorous asceticism, and fervent mysticism intimidate me, I confess. But I revere her for them. And I, like Thomas Merton and the sisters at Aywières, am charmed by her friendly, affectionate attention to others.

⟋⟍⟋

A Tiger Lily of a Saint

In the month of June, when the sun burns high in the bright firmament and when Cistercian monks, like all other farmers, hitch up their teams and go out to gather in the wheat, Saint Lutgarde's Day comes around. She is a saint whose spirit is as ardent and colorful as the June weather and as bright as the tiger lilies that enliven the fields and roadsides in the month in which we celebrate her memory.

—Thomas Merton

MIRACLES IN THE DESERT

Saint Anthony of Egypt (251—356)

※

Anthony was like a good physician given to the people of Egypt. For whoever came to him afflicted who did not go away rejoicing? Whoever came to him full of rage who was not enriched with graciousness and long-suffering? And what person ever came to him troubled in mind who did not go away with it composed? . . . People loved him so much that after he had departed from this world, his memory never died. Everyone took courage from the repetition of his triumphs and of his words.

—SAINT ATHANASIUS

Saint Anthony was not the first ascetic, but he was the first monk who fled the city to pursue God in the desert. Or perhaps to let God find and catch him there.

"Ascetic" comes from a Greek word for "athlete." Christian ascetics were spiritual athletes, and the Gospels were their workout programs. Prayer, fasting, and charitable works were their exercises. Jesus and Paul were their trainers. The Holy Spirit, as they often said, was their strength, while God was their prize, and they were his.

Anthony was born near Memphis in Egypt in 251. By then, many Christians had disengaged from ordinary life to devote themselves exclusively to God. Men and women alike had become hermits. The men were called "monks," taking their name from a Greek word for "solitary," and the women were "nuns," "nonnae" in Latin, meaning they said no to worldly desires. Some ascetics sought their solitude right in the middle of the towns. For safety's sake, the nuns stayed with their families or resided together in households, but the monks lived alone on the outskirts of cities in huts, caves, or abandoned tombs.

These ascetics pursued virtue by avoiding secular society while maintaining contact with their local Christian communities. They felt they had a lot to flee. The Roman Empire was lustful, violent, and brutish, and its culture made evil attractive. Monks and nuns abandoned these persuasively wicked environments because they believed that living apart helped them conquer their own evil tendencies.

Anthony was twenty when his parents died and left him responsible for his little sister. A few months later, at church one Sunday, a reading from the Gospels changed his life. "If you want to be perfect," proclaimed the lector, "go, sell your possessions and give to the poor, and you will have treasure in heaven. Then come, follow me" (Matthew 19:21). Anthony was certain God had spoken right to him. He responded by selling his parents' estate and the possessions he had inherited. He distributed the proceeds to the poor, reserving only enough to provide for his sister's future.

A short time later, Anthony heard another Sunday gospel declare, "Do not worry about tomorrow" (Matthew 6:34). Again, he took the words personally and gave as alms the money he had set aside for his sister. He found the little girl a home with a household of nuns, the first convent in recorded history. Then he moved to a hut on the edge of town and became a hermit. Later on, he would pursue a solitary life in the Egyptian desert.

The young monk learned the ascetical life from other recluses who lived nearby on the outskirts of the city. Imitating their Christian behavior, he diligently applied their teachings on prayer and other spiritual practices. When he noticed a virtue in one of them, he worked at acquiring it. He pursued it doggedly until he had mastered the quality even more perfectly than his model. Saint Athanasius, Anthony's biographer, said that he "was a perfect handicraftsman in matters that related to fear of God."

Anthony developed a pattern that he followed for eighty-five years. He ate once a day, never before sunset, and his meal consisted of six ounces of bread soaked in water, sometimes seasoned with a little salt. When he was elderly, he occasionally allowed himself a few palm dates and a little oil. He wore sheepskin garments with the hair against his body. Weaving mats of palm fronds was his ordinary work. Later, when he moved to the desert, he tilled a small garden, growing wheat to make his bread and vegetables for his guests.

All day and all night, Anthony prayed. At any time, a visitor might find him rapt in mystical ecstasies. He loved to pray at night and sometimes complained that the sunrise robbed him of the greater light of inner contemplation.

Once, however, he became depressed because he did not feel strong enough for lengthy prayer. He took comfort from a vision in which an angel showed him the value of balancing prayer and work. The angel alternately wove mats and then rose to pray. After a while, the angel said, "Do this, and you will find relief." So the saint adjusted his pattern. However, Saint Athanasius says, he continued to pray a little while he worked.

Anthony's monastic career progressed through three stages. For fifteen years he lived in huts and tombs near the village of Koman. Then, at age thirty-five, he withdrew to an isolated mountain in the Egyptian desert to escape the steady stream of people who sought him for miraculous cures. After twenty years, however, he entered a more active phase and left his mountain retreat to form communities of hermits in the desert. Occasionally he traveled into Alexandria to lend his personal support to the local Christians, who faced both persecution and heresy.

Saint Athanasius reported that the devil opposed Anthony at every turn throughout his life. As a result, the saint became adept at spiritual warfare. As a young monk, he valiantly resisted temptations to lust and second thoughts about his vocation. The enemy also attacked Anthony by appearing in visible forms, once as a woman and then again as a strong young man. But the saint typically overcame the devil's phantasms by proclaiming the name of Jesus.

Athanasius said that once when Anthony had gone into the desert, the devil sent an army of wild animals against him. As they were about to pounce, the saint confronted them. "If the Lord has given you power over me," he shouted, "come and get it over with. But if Satan sent you, get out of here quickly, for I am a servant of Jesus." At the name of *Jesus*, the animals scattered. And, said Athanasius, Satan was driven away "like a sparrow before a hawk."

All of Egypt knew about Anthony's power over the devil, and so many people flocked to him, seeking deliverance from evil spirits. Anthony, however, diverted attention from his gifts by requiring petitioners to exercise their own faith. Once Martinianus, a Roman official, asked him to release his daughter from obsession by a demon. "Why do you bother me?" said Anthony. "I'm a man, just like you. But if you believe in Christ, whom I serve, go away and you'll receive your request." As Martinianus and his child were on their way home, the girl was touched by the supernatural and set free.

On another occasion, Parnîtôn, also an official, came with the claim that a demon was causing him to gnaw his tongue and to lose his sight. He wanted to stay with Anthony until he was healed, but the Saint ordered him to leave. "You can't be healed here," he said. "Go back to Egypt. There you will see the wonderful sign God has worked for you." Parnîtôn obeyed, and before he reached home he was cured.

Anthony claimed no supernatural gift of healing, only inspired knowledge of God's interventions in someone's life. Once, a nun from the region of Busiris whose face was so afflicted with cancer that she had gone blind longed for Anthony to pray for her. Some relatives took her and joined company with a group of monks who were crossing the desert to visit the saint. When the entourage drew near the mountain where Anthony lived, the family and the nun stayed behind while the monks went on to see him. Awestruck in Anthony's presence, the monks were hesitant to ask him do something for the young woman. But the saint miraculously read their thoughts. Before they could say a word about her, he startled them by saying, "Go back to the place where you left the maiden, and you will find that she has been healed completely. This didn't happen through me or through any gift of mine. It's a gift from God, who heard the young lady's prayer and saw the faithful concern of her family. He revealed to me just now that he has cured her." Quickly, the monks returned to find the family celebrating gaily and the young nun's body restored, clean of any trace of cancer.

When he turned fifty-five, Saint Anthony left the seclusion of his mountain retreat to found a monastic settlement. It was an informal community of solitaries who built huts near to each other.

A community of solitaries. That sounds like an oxymoron, doesn't it? It's a contradiction, however, only if we imagine that in his flight to the desert, Anthony rejected all relationships. Though he valued his solitude, he welcomed those who sought him out. Many ordinary people looking for miracles tracked him down in the most remote places. Monks came in large numbers to learn from him. Their appeals for help seem to have persuaded him to build a community in the wilderness.

Anthony's monks dwelled apart, but gathered for prayer and teaching. Living alone together enabled them to help each other in their quest for holiness. According to Athanasius, Anthony taught his community about faith, love of God, discipline of the flesh, prayer, Scripture study, and reflection. The heart of his teaching, however, was instruction on loving one another, forgiveness, avoiding and repairing wrongdoing, and mutual accountability. Anthony wanted his brothers both to prize their relationship with God and to support it by learning to love one another.

Anthony also had a brotherly commitment to the Christians of Alexandria, with whom he was in regular contact. He was the loyal friend of Saint Athanasius, the bishop who wrote his life story. In 311, when the Roman Empire renewed its persecution of Christians, Anthony went to Alexandria to encourage the martyrs. Fearlessly, he put himself at great risk by appearing in the presence of the governor. Friends finally persuaded him to leave so as not to provoke an attack on himself.

Later, he used his immense popularity to oppose the Arian heresy. In the 330s, the Arians, who held that Jesus was a creature and not God, were making inroads in Alexandria. At Athanasius's urging, in 339 Anthony came to the city to speak against the heresy. Crowds rallied around him, and he warned them to shun the heretics that they might not be led astray by their errors.

After this foray into the city, Saint Anthony returned to the desert. He longed for the solitude and opportunities for contemplation. However, so many people sought his help that he was hardly ever alone. At the request of some monks, he founded another monastery. Officials came to consult him, philosophers to debate him, and petitioners to be healed. The saint spent his last years loving God by loving others.

Remarkably, Saint Anthony's lifelong austerity does not seem to have damaged his body. Even in his old age he appeared strong. "His eyes did not wax dim," said Saint Athanasius, "and not one of his teeth dropped out, and both his feet and his hands were sound and healthy. Even though he ate so little, his appearance was more glorious than that of those who fed themselves on dainty meats."

Not bad for a very old monk who reportedly had fasted every day for eighty-five years.

⚬⚬⚬

Acquiring Virtue

Let us continue to be strenuous in the pursuit of virtue. Let us not grow tired of seeking it, for our Lord has become a guide for us and for every person who has a desire for the virtues. And so that it might not be tedious for us, Saint Paul became our example when he said, "I die daily" (1 Corinthians 15:31). Now, if we were to think each day that we had to die that day, we would never sin at all. This is the explanation of Paul's saying. . . . If we were to keep the imminence of our death in mind, we would never be overcome by sin: lust which is fleeting would not reign over us; we would never harbor anger against another human being; we would not love the possessions which pass away; and we would forgive every person who offended us. . . . Therefore, O my beloved, let us be zealous in carrying out the work we have committed ourselves to, and let us travel to the end on the road on which we have begun our journey.

—SAINT ATHANASIUS

ROYAL MIRACLES

Saint Elizabeth of Hungary (1207–1231)

❦

*Is not this the kind of fasting I have chosen: to loose the chains of injustice . . .
to set the oppressed free? . . . Is it not to share your food with the hungry and
to provide the poor wanderer with shelter. . . . Then your light will break forth
like the dawn, and your healing will quickly appear; then your righteousness
will go before you, and the glory of the LORD will be your rear guard.*
—ISAIAH 58:6–8

Elizabeth of Hungary was a wife, mother, activist, mystic, and miracle worker, and in her short life, she accomplished far more than
most of us ever do. And she did it amid stressful hardships.

Elizabeth was the daughter of King Andrew II of Hungary and
Gertrude, his queen. As a child, she was betrothed to Ludwig, the son of
Hermann, the count of Thuringia, and at age four, she was sent to Wart-
burg Castle to be reared with her future husband. Two years later, her
mother was cruelly murdered by the king's enemies.

The count's greedy courtiers hated the princess because she gave so
much to the poor, and they treated her rudely. But Ludwig grew fond of

Elizabeth and eventually fell in love with her. When the young man traveled, he brought his betrothed little gifts—a string of beads, a bag, or gloves. She would run out to meet him, and he would take her on his arm and give her the present.

When Elizabeth was fourteen and Ludwig was twenty-one, he succeeded his father as the count of Thuringia. Against the advice of his counselors, he married his beloved princess. "I would rather cast away a mountain of gold," he said, "than give her up." Over the next six years the happy couple had three children.

Ludwig regarded Elizabeth as his special pearl, and he encouraged her pursuit of holiness. Elizabeth arranged for her handmaids to awaken her for prayer during the night without disturbing Ludwig. Sometimes, however, when they thought the count was sleeping, he was merely playing possum. Once, a maid thought she was gently shaking her mistress, only to find she had taken hold of Ludwig's foot. The frightened young lady explained herself, and Ludwig, perhaps with a sleepy smile, let it pass.

Courtiers regularly criticized Elizabeth for her generous giving to the poor. In 1225, Thuringia suffered a grievous famine. To provide for the suffering, she exhausted her own financial resources and her grain supply. But when household officers complained to Ludwig, he brushed them off. "Has she disposed of any of my lands?" he asked.

"No," answered the saint's critics.

"Then you have no complaint," he said. "As for her charities, they will bring us God's blessing."

With her husband's approval, Elizabeth then constructed a hospital. To make it accessible to the poor, she located it at the base of the rock atop which the unapproachable castle was built. Elizabeth visited the hospital twice daily so that she could personally minister to the sick. She also fed nine hundred people every day, plus providing for large numbers of the hungry throughout Thuringia. To encourage responsibility among those she served, she gave them opportunities to work as the requirement for receiving her aid.

One morning she found a deformed boy lying on the hospital's threshold. The child was deaf and dumb and so disabled that he could barely drag himself along the ground. His mother had left him at the door, hoping that Elizabeth could help him.

The saint did not know of the child's impairments and tried to speak with him.

"Dear child, who brought you here?" she asked.

No answer.

"From what are you suffering? Will you not answer me?"

Again, no response.

She took pity on the boy, thinking that some demon was at the root of his ailments. "In the name of our Lord," she said loudly, "I command you, and him that is in you, to reply and to tell me where you came from!"

At that, the boy stood up, completely restored to health. Even though he had never spoken before, he could now explain his situation—how his mother had brought him to the hospital and that he had been deaf, dumb, feeble, and deformed from birth. The princess asked him to keep her role in his healing as a little secret between the two of them, but he told his mother, and she told everyone she could. So the saint's gift of healing became widely known, and many came seeking her gracious touch.

On another occasion, when Elizabeth was praying at a church near the hospital, she saw a blind man feeling his way about the building. She watched as he slowly moved his hands over the face of a statue of Mary and smiled fondly in recognition.

"Why are you wandering around the church?" asked the saint.

"I came to find the lady who helps the poor," he said. "First, I came to pray in the church. Now I am going around to feel how long and wide it is."

"Would you like to see the church?" she asked.

"God willing," he said. "But I was born blind."

"Maybe it's best you were blind," said Elizabeth. "You might have fallen into something worse."

"Oh, no," he said. "I would have been glad to work, like everybody else."

"Pray that God will give you light," she said, "and I will pray for you." She knelt nearby and prayed, and as she did, the man received his sight. The two of them celebrated by taking a tour of the church.

Once Elizabeth put a leper in the bed that she and her husband shared. Not surprisingly, Ludwig was enraged. He ran into the room and pulled back the blankets. Instead of seeing a leper, however, the count had a vision of the crucified Christ lying on the bed. From then on, he let his wife freely pursue her service to the poor and the sick.

In 1227, Ludwig and his army joined a crusade to the Holy Land. He got as far as Otranto, in southern Italy, where he contracted the plague and died. Elizabeth had just given birth to her third child, a daughter, when the news reached Thuringia. At the age of twenty, she had become a widow. In her grief, she is said to have shrieked like a madwoman and run wildly about the castle. "The world is dead to me," she cried, "and all that was joyous in the world."

The last years of Elizabeth's life were anything but peaceful. Though the facts are unclear, it seems that her husband's relatives forced her from her home. At the same time, she was receiving spiritual direction from Master Conrad of Marburg, a mean-spirited priest who strove to break the saint's will in order to foster her sanctity. He even forced her to send away the maids who had served her lifelong, thus depriving her of the intimate friends she loved the most.

Despite her bitter losses, the young princess endured. She joined the Third Order of Saint Francis, the association of laypeople who patterned their lives on his rule. Then she built herself a little house in Marburg, where she lived austerely and continued her ministry to the needy. To earn money for her charity, she fished in the streams, carded wool, and spun cloth. Increasingly, she gave herself over to prayer.

Elizabeth prayed many hours at a time in church. However, she especially liked to pray in the fields. Her favorite place was in the woods at a clear fountain at the foot of a rugged hill. It is said that she even prayed through driving rain without getting wet.

The saint frequently prayed for others to experience God. Once she spoke with Berthold, a boy of fourteen, about his extravagant dress.

"Do you think the Savior would have dressed in suede as you do?" she asked.

The lad dodged the question. "Dear lady," he said, "why don't you just pray for me? Maybe I'd change and want to serve God."

"Do you really want me to pray for you?" asked Elizabeth.

"Yes, I do," said Berthold.

Young Berthold seems to have gotten more than he bargained for. As Elizabeth prayed, something extraordinary happened. "Stop, ma'am!" he cried. "I can't stand it any longer! My body is all inflamed!" But she kept on praying until he said he thought his heart would break. Afterward, the young man's behavior revealed that the experience had indeed had a significant spiritual effect on him. Ultimately, he became a member of the Friars Minor, the religious order of Saint Francis of Assisi.

More and more, Elizabeth progressed in mystical prayer. Frequently, she appeared to lose consciousness for long periods. These deep prayer times strengthened her body, and when she emerged from them, she had no need of food. When asked to express how she felt in her ecstasy, she could only respond with a paraphrased line from the *Song of Songs*: "My soul fainted away when my beloved spoke to me" (see chapter 5, verse 6).

The saint lived only two years at Marburg before her health declined. At dawn on November 17, 1231, Elizabeth spoke softly to her attendant, "It is now the time of day when the Lord rose from the grave and broke the doors of hell, and he will release me." The princess died that evening at twenty-four years of age.

෴

The Princess of the Poor

Acting as a true child of the gospel, Elizabeth saw in the person of her neighbor the divine Jesus, the only object of her affection. She loved him with so admirable a charity that her delight was to see herself surrounded by the poor, to live and converse with them. She most dearly cherished those whose misery and disgusting maladies rendered them most horrible, and whose appearance would be sufficient to terrify the strongest hearts in the world. She so charitably distributed all her wealth among them that she left herself poor and indigent to supply all things necessary for them in abundance. She was but of that youthful age when children still require instructors, and already she was the good mother, the guardian and protectress of the poor, and her heart was full of compassion for their sufferings.

—POPE GREGORY IX

Miracles to the Rescue

Saint Clare of Assisi (1193 – 1253)

ⴷⵎⵓ

*What are the servants of God but his singers whose duty it is
to lift up the hearts of men and women and move them to spiritual joy?*
—SAINT FRANCIS OF ASSISI

A popular notion imagines that Saint Clare and Saint Francis of Assisi were romantically linked. *Brother Sun and Sister Moon,* a silly movie, helped spread this nonsense. It may make good fiction, but let's set the record straight.

Clare and Francis were not lovers.

They were not infatuated with each other.

Clare and Francis did not "hang out" together.

And they never slipped away for lovers' rendezvous.

If you are looking for a medieval couple who were a "thing," stick with Heloise and Abelard.

Eighteen-year-old Clare encountered Francis for the first time when she heard him preach at Saint George's in Assisi. At the time, Clare was already a devoted Christian, but Francis' plain talk about Christ's love intensified her desire to live more fully for God. She decided she would find a way to imitate the saint's gospel pattern of life.

Clare met with Francis numerous times, always in the company of a close female friend. Their visits were clandestine, so as not to alarm her family. Clare's parents were notables in Assisi, and they expected her to marry well. The saint knew that once her spiritual intentions were public her family would raise a furious storm of resistance. One relative, Rufino, had already disgraced the family by joining Francis' band of beggars. Clare knew that her relatives would view her decision as an even more dishonorable defection. She would be throwing away her chance to advance the family's fortunes. Worse, she would be disgracing them by joining a disreputable movement that associated with Assisi's underclass.

Francis and Clare evidently agreed that she would start a women's community modeled on his friars. Very likely they consulted Bishop Guido of Assisi about Clare's vocation. He was Francis' early, enthusiastic protector, and the saint always sought his direction.

Palm Sunday, 1212, was set as the date that Clare would flee her family. That morning, she attended the liturgy as usual. Thomas of Celano, her biographer, says Clare was "resplendent with joy." He hinted that Clare regarded that Mass as her marriage to Christ. When everyone went forward to receive palm fronds, she stayed back with a bride's shyness. Bishop Guido noticed and carried a branch to her. Perhaps he winked his complicity as he offered her this little sign of encouragement.

In the evening, accompanied by a relative, Clare slipped away from her parents' home. Francis and his brothers welcomed her at the church of Saint Mary of the Angels. Bearing torches and singing the *Veni Creator Spiritus*, they proceeded into the chapel. There Clare made her profession. "I want only Jesus Christ," she said, "and to live by the Gospel, owning nothing and in chastity." Francis sealed her vow by shearing her long, golden hair, and Clare traded her clothing for a coarse sackcloth habit.

Then the trouble began, as Clare's departure had precipitated a great scandal in Assisi. Decent but worldly people were enraged, judging her as selfish and headstrong. For Clare's security, Francis hid her nearby in a Benedictine convent. When her powerful uncle, Monaldo, discovered her whereabouts, he and a posse of her male relatives tried to forcibly remove her and bring her home. The angry men burst into the convent, where they found Clare in the chapel, clinging to the altar. She felt she would be safe there because they would be reluctant to invade the sanctuary and thus defile it. Finally, to show that nothing could make her change her mind, Clare startled the men by uncovering her shorn head. At that, her would-be kidnappers admitted the hopelessness of their effort and left.

A few days later, Agnes, Clare's fifteen-year-old sister, joined her at the convent. Shamed even more by the flight of one so young, an enraged Monaldo and his men again stormed the convent, demanding to see Agnes. Then, when the frightened girl appeared, Monaldo shouted, "What do you think you are doing? You will come home with me right now!"

"I have decided to follow Christ and his gospel with Clare," said Agnes. "I will never leave her."

At that, the men grabbed her and dragged her from the convent. Agnes screamed for help, neighbors came running, and Clare knelt in prayer. Then a marvelous thing happened in the sight of all. When one of the men stooped to lift Agnes and carry her off, he could not budge her. By divine intervention the girl had become so heavy that no one could move her. Exasperated, the men finally gave up. Clare's prayer had conquered them and they left, never to return.

Francis gave Clare a little house contiguous with the vacant church of Saint Damian on the outskirts of Assisi. This became the base from which the saint built her community. Women from prominent local families soon joined her, Clare's mother among them. Within a few years, convents of Clare's sisters opened in Italy and France. Even Agnes of Bohemia renounced her proposed marriage to the Emperor Frederick II to found a convent in that country.

Clare and her sisters joyfully lived a penitential life. They wore rough clothing, went barefoot, slept on the ground, fasted frequently, never ate meat, and never spoke unless it was necessary. Clare was devoted to "Lady Poverty." She wanted her community to own nothing and live on daily contributions.

Though Clare of Assisi is not known as a miracle worker, God intervened in events on her behalf. Once the convent was out of oil, a minor disaster in any Italian household. Clare washed a jar and placed it at the door. When the friar who begged on behalf of the sisters came for it, he was surprised to find it full of oil. On another occasion, Clare fed fifty sisters and all the friars with a single loaf of bread.

The saint was also blessed with a gift of healing. Thomas of Celano said that when Clare called upon the power of the crucified Christ she could make people's maladies disappear. Once Saint Francis sent Stephen, a friar who was mentally ill, to Clare. She touched him, and he immediately recovered his senses. Three-year-old Mattiolo was brought to Clare, a pebble lodged in his nostril. When she blessed him in the name of Christ, the stone fell out.

Clare also healed her sisters—Benevenuta, who had suffered twelve years with open sores; Amata, of edema; Christiana, of deafness. One night another Benevenuta, who was without her voice for two years, had a vision that Clare would heal her the next day, and Clare did. On another occasion Clare walked into the infirmary, called on the power of the Cross, and five sisters were immediately cured of their diseases.

Twice Clare's courage and intercession miraculously saved Assisi. In 1241, Emperor Frederick II invaded northern Italy. Among the imperial troops were Saracens who ravaged the Spoleto valley where Assisi lay. Saint Damian was an easy target, sitting exposed on the edge of the town. Clare, although very sick, took bold action to defend her sisters. The saint confronted the raiders at the door with a silver box containing a consecrated host.

Prostrating herself, she prayed: "Does it please you, Lord, to deliver your defenseless handmaids into the hands of these pagans? I beg you, Lord, defend them for me, since I can't defend them myself." She also prayed for the protection of Assisi. Then a voice was heard to say, "I will always defend you," and at that the marauders clambered over the walls and fled.

Shortly after that, a general in the imperial army besieged Assisi. When it appeared that the city would fall, Clare and her sisters once again interceded for it. They removed their veils, covered their heads with ashes, and pleaded for the city's safety. Their prayer was answered swiftly. Overnight the army disbanded, and not long after, the general was killed.

For the last two decades of her life Clare, the saint who cured others, was very sick. But she endured her infirmities with remarkable fortitude. Once, when a brother exhorted her to patience, she asserted candidly: "Ever since I have known the grace of my Lord Jesus Christ through his servant Francis, no suffering has troubled me, no penance has been hard, no sickness too arduous." She died in 1253.

Clare believed that her life and the lives of her sisters were "patterns and mirrors for those who live in the world." Do you see in her, as I do, a luminous reflection of Christ?

꧁

The Spotless Mirror

Happy the soul to whom it is given to attain this life with Christ, to cleave with all one's heart to Him:

Whose beauty all the heavenly hosts behold forever,
Whose love inflames our love,
Whose contemplation is our refreshment,
Whose graciousness is our delight,
Whose gentleness fills us to overflowing,
Whose remembrance gives sweet light,
Whose fragrance revives the dead,
Whose glorious vision will be the happiness of all the citizens of
    that heavenly Jerusalem.

For he is the brightness of eternal glory (Hebrews 1:3), the splendor of eternal light, the mirror without spot (Wisdom 7:26).

—Saint Clare of Assisi

Part Three

⌘

Miracles of Conversion

Go into all the world and preach
the good news to all creation.
Whoever believes and is baptized
will be saved, but whoever does not
believe will be condemned. And
these signs will accompany those
who believe: In my name they will
drive out demons; they will speak
in new tongues; they will pick
up snakes with their hands; and
when they drink deadly poison,
it will not hurt them at all; they
will place their hands on sick
people, and they will get well.

—MARK 16:15–18

Christ's first public miracle was one of conversion. At the wedding of Cana he converted water into wine because his mother asked him to (see John 2:1–11). Among my favorite persons in the Bible are those unnamed waiters who did what Jesus told them to do and lugged six huge water jars, placing them before him. I admire them because by simply following Christ's directions they became collaborators in a remarkable wonder. Those servants seem to me to be prototypes of the saints from whose obedience miracles also flowed.

Perhaps the conversion of water to wine hinted at another more fundamental Christian miracle of conversion, the transformation of human beings into children of God. Again, I think that also points to the saints. Exemplars of conversion themselves, they were dedicated to helping others enter the Christian miracle and become transformed in Christ. The miracle of personal conversion lies at the heart of Christianity and sums up what Christians call the "Good News." This miracle, in fact, is the message.

Through the ages, the saints' exemplary lives have broadcast the Christian promise of conversion. The relentless generosity of saints like Martin and Elizabeth showed the world that it had been touched by the supernatural. The saints' unremitting kindness defies mere human explanations. Their unselfish goodness so repels our natural selfishness that we must suspect it has a divine source. No one can be that good all the time on his or her own strength. The miracles that poured from the saints' charity confirmed that a supernatural impulse quickened them. Thus, the miracle of their lives is their message.

The example of the martyrs is an even more convincing testimony to the Christian Gospel. Observers had to be moved by the courage of saints like Apphian and Sabas. They had to be curious about these young men who embraced death so willingly. How could they freely choose the thing most repugnant to human beings? Onlookers must have toyed with this question: Either Apphian and Sabas were touched by madness or they were touched by God. The miracles that attended their martyrdom argued in favor of a divine touch.

Saints who were preachers or teachers played a special role in communicating the Christian message of conversion. Some, like Anthony of Padua, were gifted with dynamic eloquence. A medieval forerunner of Billy Graham, he attracted and swayed thousands wherever he went. Some, like Dominic, were strategic speakers. He not only dazzled crowds by confronting and confuting heretics, but he also multiplied his influence by training a band of gifted men in his style and methods. Visions and dreams guided both Dominic and Anthony, and miracles authenticated their preaching. Major players in the extraordinary spiritual renewal of the thirteenth century, the arrival of these exceptional men on that scene seems in itself miraculous.

And then there's Saint Vincent Ferrer, who may be in a class all by himself. Preacher, diplomat, visionary, healer, wonder-worker—you name it, he seems to have done it all. Simply put, Saint Vincent Ferrer's life was a continuous miracle of conversion. If you are familiar with him, you know what I mean. If you are not, you will get to know him in later chapters.

⁖⁖⁖

Miracles in Action

Saint Dominic (1170–1221)

༺∞༠

*In the presence of a significant life, we behold not only our own life
as it is but possibilities and potential for the future.*
—Anthony Padovano

Saint Dominic was a carefully crafted arrow strategically aimed at the thirteenth century. "Carefully crafted," because his education and training specifically prepared him for a life's work he did not anticipate. "Strategically aimed," because he struck at the heart of problems afflicting the church and the world of his day. And history shows that he was right on target.

Joan of Aza, Dominic's mother, was a remarkable woman on her own account. Later beatified by the Roman Catholic Church, she had several visions that predicted her son's significant work. Before Dominic was born, she dreamed that she would bear a son who would be a shining light to the church. During her pregnancy, Joan also dreamed that she bore a dog in her womb and that it broke away from her with a burning torch in its mouth by which it set fire to the world.

Dominic was born around 1170 at Calaruega in Castile. Just before his baptism, Joan had a third prophetic dream. On her baby's forehead appeared a bright star that enlightened the world. Now, granted, many mothers have big dreams for their infants. Mostly, however, these are merely hopes that may or may not be realized. But Joan's dreams were revelations that came true.

When Dominic was seven, Joan sent him to study with his uncle, the parish priest at Gumiel d'Izan. At fourteen, he enrolled in the University of Palencia. There Dominic completed his secular studies within six years. Then he devoted four years to the study of theology.

Jordan of Saxony, the saint's first biographer, tells us that during these years Dominic immersed himself in Scripture. He studied it thoroughly, diligently recording his teacher's insights in the margins of his parchment copy of the Bible.

For Dominic, however, acting on Scripture was more important than studying it. In 1195, Spain was ravaged by war and famine, and impoverished refugees poured into Palencia. Moved by their plight, Dominic sold all his possessions in order to contribute to their relief. He even sold his precious parchments. "I will not study on dead skins," he said, "when others are dying of hunger."

Dominic's generous example caught the attention of Diego of Acebo, the prior of the chapter at Osma. A chapter was a religious community of men, usually located at a cathedral church. Its members were called "canons" because they lived according to a rule or canon. Diego was recruiting talented young men for his diocese, and he had his bishop invite Dominic to join his community of clerics. Thus in 1195, at age twenty-five, Dominic became a canon of the cathedral at Osma. Within the year he was ordained a priest.

Diego's community had adopted the Rule of Saint Augustine, which incorporated many features of early Christian piety. Daily observance of that life pattern for nine years completed Dominic's formation. At Osma, the saint mastered the spiritual disciplines of prayer and self-denial. Dominic prayed many hours each day, sometimes long into the night. He was often observed weeping for sinners and for the afflicted. Jordan said that Dominic "was persuaded that he could not truly be a member of Christ unless he consecrated himself wholly to the work of gaining souls." It would not be long before Dominic got his heart's desire.

Diego became bishop of Osma in 1201, and Dominic succeeded him as prior of the chapter. Three years later, King Alphonsus IX of Castile sent Bishop Diego to Denmark to arrange a marriage for his son, and Diego took Dominic along as his companion. That mission occasioned a major shift in the saint's life from a predominantly contemplative phase to a predominantly active one.

Their journey took Diego and Dominic through Languedoc, a stronghold of the Albigensians. That sect had won many converts in southern France and northern Italy. In contrast to a somewhat decadent Christian clergy, the Albigensian leaders seemed to be paragons of virtue. People were attracted to their rigorously simple lifestyle. Rooted in ancient Eastern religions, Albigensians proclaimed a stark dualism, holding that everything material is evil, and everything spiritual is good. They denied the humanity of Christ because they believed that a wicked body could not contain God's pure spirit. Their prohibition of all procreation and their endorsement of suicide threatened ordinary society.

When the party stopped at Toulouse, Dominic was housed at an inn with an Albigensian host. The saint spent the night patiently persuading the man that his beliefs were false. The next morning, the innkeeper renounced his errors and returned to the Christian faith. That event foreshadowed Dominic's future service, as he seemed ideally equipped to help turn the Albigensian tide. Dominic himself did not see it at first. Pursuing their dream of Christianizing the Tartars, he and Diego continued on to Rome to ask Pope Innocent III's leave to preach the Gospel in Russia. But the pope had other ideas. He charged them to return to Languedoc to assist in the recovery of Christians who had fallen prey to the Albigensians.

Back in France, Dominic and Diego confirmed their suspicions about the failure of efforts against the heresy. Dominic observed that the clergy leading the campaign appeared lax and wealthy. They were no match for the austere sect leaders. He recommended that all preachers win the right to be heard by imitating the self-denial of their opponents. He also believed that gentle persuasion rather than vigorous condemnation was the way to turn Albigensians to the Christian faith.

In 1206, Dominic and Diego engaged in a series of disputations with Albigensian leaders. The most memorable of these was held at Fanjeux in Languedoc, where both sides agreed to accept the decision of a panel of lay judges. Each group prepared a written summary of their strongest arguments. Dominic prepared the church's case. After reviewing the presentations, the judges refused to decide. Instead, they demanded a trial by fire, a not-unusual practice at the time.

An official threw the documents, one at a time, into a great bonfire. The Albigensian case was first. The onlookers watched in stony silence as the flames hungrily consumed it. But Dominic's book was mysteriously thrust out of the flames, intact. "Hurrah!" someone shouted, and the astonished crowd began to cheer. Not satisfied with the result, the judges repeated the trial. Once again the official submitted both documents to the blaze. It was a repeat performance—the Albigensian book was reduced to ashes, and Dominic's emerged unharmed. Greatly entertained by this wonder, the crowd hooted its approval. Even though Dominic had already won the best out of three, the judges ran the test again. And a third time, Dominic's book triumphed. The onlookers guffawed, and some of them sniped jokes at the Albigensians. This triple miracle, however, did not convince the saint's opponents. They reneged on the agreement to accept the judges' decision and suppressed news of the wonder.

Such debates accomplished little in the battle against the Albigensians. Dominic would achieve much more through the creation of his communities of men and women. By their word and example these dedicated believers would change hearts throughout Europe.

Dominic conceived a plan to raise up counterorganizations against the highly structured sect. In contrast to the heretics, the saint thought the church appeared to be in disarray. He decided that since people seemed attracted to the community life of the Albigensians, the church must create similar communities that would draw them back. Perhaps the idea first came to the saint when he observed the success of the sect's well-organized schools, which the heretics used to recruit young women. As an alternative, Dominic wanted to establish a sisterhood of Catholic women who could offer a safe education for girls.

One night in July 1206, Dominic was resting on a hill near Fanjeux overlooking the little village of Prouille. He enjoyed the cool breeze that rustled the trees and refreshed him with the fragrance of the grass and summer flowers. Gazing at the moonlit houses all quieted for the night, he drifted into prayer. As he watched, a fiery globe seemed to descend from the heavens and rest over a chapel dedicated to Mary. Dominic interpreted this vision as a sign from God that he was to establish a community of women at the church of Our Lady of Prouille.

Dominic's first sisters were nine former Albigensians who were converted by his preaching. He provided them a simple rule of life and charged them to run a school for girls. He also directed them to pray for the work of preaching. On December 27, 1206, the women took up residence at the Prouille church.

Nearby, Dominic opened a house for his associates, men carefully chosen for their gifts and specially trained as preachers. Thus Dominic laid the groundwork for what would become his gift to the church—religious communities that would revolutionize the world through prayer, preaching, and education.

At Rome in 1215, Dominic sought Pope Innocent III's official approval for his projects. The pope readily authorized the Prouille sisterhood, but he was reluctant to give approval to the Friars Preachers because the bishops at the Fourth Lateran Council had recently ruled against the multiplication of new religious orders. Then, in a dream, the pope saw Dominic holding up the collapsing basilica of Saint John Lateran. Moved by the vision, he encouraged Dominic to dodge the council's decision by choosing an existing religious rule for his brothers. In August 1216, Dominic and sixteen associates met at Prouille and adopted the Rule of Saint Augustine. The following October, Dominic returned to Rome where Pope Honorius III, Innocent's successor, gave final approval for the Friars Preachers.

It is said that while in Rome, Dominic had a vision in which Mary showed Jesus two figures whose work would spare the world from God's wrath. He recognized himself as one. In church the next day, he identified an unkempt beggar as the other. He embraced Francis of Assisi and said, "You are my companion. You must walk with me." So the two great men became friends.

On August 13, 1217, Dominic met with his friars at Prouille. He instructed them in his methods of preaching, exhorting them to put a priority on holiness and on study. He also spoke about humility, faith, endurance, and spiritual warfare. Then, two days later, to the surprise of all, Dominic divided his little community, dispersing brothers all over Europe. "Leave it to me," he said. "I know what I'm about. We must sow the seed, not hoard it." Seven brothers went to Paris, four to Spain, two to Toulouse, and two remained at Prouille. Dominic and a companion returned to Rome, where he hoped at last to get the pope's permission to evangelize the Tartars. But it was not to be.

At Rome, the pope commissioned Dominic to establish a group of friars at the church of Saint Sixtus. The pope also assigned him to conduct a reformation among certain nuns scattered throughout Rome and living without much supervision. While he was about these tasks, two famous miracles occurred.

The Rome foundation of Friars Preachers grew quickly. By 1219, about forty men resided at Saint Sixtus. One day when there was no food in the house, two brothers were sent to beg. Near the end of the day, all they had received was one loaf of bread. When a beggar approached them for alms, the friars gave it to him. They returned home empty-handed. When Dominic heard their report, he said, "It was an angel of the Lord. The Lord knows how to provide for his own. Let's go and pray." Dominic prayed briefly in the church, then with the brothers in the refectory. After Dominic blessed the friars, two handsome young men appeared. They carried bread in two white cloths that hung from their shoulders. Beginning at the lowest table and ending with Dominic, they distributed a loaf to each brother. Then, just as mysteriously as they had arrived, they disappeared. Dominican houses still commemorate this miracle daily; food is distributed first to the lay brothers, from the youngest to the most senior.

By Lent 1219, with grace and diplomacy, Dominic had persuaded forty-four sisters in Rome to unite in one community. He gave the nuns

Saint Sixtus, and the pope assigned him a new center for the friars. Dominic and three cardinals received the sisters' profession on Ash Wednesday. During the ceremony, word came that Napoleon, a nephew of one of the cardinals, had fallen from his horse and died.

Dominic had the corpse carried into the chapel. Then he assembled the cardinals, nuns, and friars and celebrated Mass. When he finished, he stood over Napoleon's broken body and arranged the limbs properly. The saint blessed the corpse, and with hands raised to heaven, he shouted, "Napoleon, in the name of our Lord Jesus Christ, arise." Immediately, in view of many reliable witnesses, the young man arose, sound and whole. Amazed and delighted, the cardinals and many others greeted him with affectionate embraces.

During these years, Dominic visited friaries throughout Europe. He had been right about scattering the seed. By 1221, when the saint died, he had sixty friaries that were divided into eight provinces. The Friars Preachers were, at that time, in France, Italy, Spain, and England and had gone to Poland, Scandinavia, and the Holy Land.

For a long time I have believed that spiritual health depends on paying attention to a few essentials. Spending daily time in prayer. Regular study. Participation in a community. Reaching out to others. I struggle to make these activities part of my own life. I look back and realize that too often I have neglected one or another of them. Saint Dominic, on the other hand, practiced all these essentials until they became second nature to him. Perhaps that's why he could respond so readily and effectively to God's call. As I reflect on his life, my hope is revived that even in my late middle age I can acquire the spiritual disciplines. I'm smart enough to know that all the hard work in the world won't "earn" me a touch of the supernatural. If the Holy Spirit is going to strike, I want to be a ready target. And prayer, study, and the like can put me right on the bull's-eye.

൭ഝൕൟ

On Self-Control

A man who governs his passions is master of the world. We must either rule them, or be ruled by them. It is better to be the hammer than the anvil.

—SAINT DOMINIC

Miracles in Death

Saint Sabas and Saint Apphian (fourth century)

What saint has ever won his crown without first contending for it?
—Saint Jerome

Christianity spread throughout the world by word and by deed and especially by the example of martyrs.

Personally, I am particularly moved by young martyrs like Saint Perpetua, who had convincing reasons to live—families, babies, position, wealth, comforts. The same was true of Saint Sabas and Saint Apphian. They were twenty-year-olds with their whole lives ahead of them. Yet they abandoned it all, and their deaths proclaimed their faith to everyone they left behind. And miracles occurred that affirmed these youthful martyrs.

We know little about Saint Sabas's life. However, we have a detailed account of his martyrdom and of the miracles surrounding his death.

In the mid-fourth century, marauding Goths made occasional raids into Asia Minor. They captured Christians there and brought them back as slaves to their bases in the northeastern Roman Empire. The captives soon converted some of their masters, and Christian communities developed among the Goths. In 370, a Gothic commander launched a persecution of Christians in his region. Over several years, fifty-one Goths were martyred. Sabas was the most famous of these.

He converted to Christianity as a boy and served the church as cantor for a priest named Sansala. During the persecution, the magistrates ordered Christians to eat meat offered to pagan gods, a practice the church condemned as idolatry. Some pagan Goths tried to protect their Christian relatives with a subterfuge, secretly arranging for them to be served meat that had not been sacrificed.

Sabas, however, would have none of this trickery. Not only did he repudiate the ruse by refusing to eat at all, but he publicly rebuked those who submitted to it as having betrayed Christ. The persecutors ignored him, but he caught their attention again the following year. To defend family and friends, some leaders of his town gathered before an imperial official to swear falsely that no Christians lived there. Sabas boldly interrupted the proceedings. "Let no one swear for me!" he shouted. "I am a Christian." Once again he escaped punishment because the official judged that the poor young man was not influential enough to cause any real harm.

It was not long before the persecution escalated. Shortly after Easter, Atharidus, a Gothic commander, and his soldiers came to town. One night they broke into Sansala and Sabas's house and carried the priest off in a cart. After beating Sabas with clubs, they dragged him naked over thorn bushes. The ardent youth may have received this special treatment because he had not shown the soldiers much respect.

The next morning the brash saint taunted his torturers. "Didn't you drag me naked over thorns? Check me over! Look and see if my feet are wounded. See if your blows left any bruises on my body." They examined

him and found not a mark, as the saint had either bee[...]
miraculously healed.

Furious, the soldiers decided to make Sabas suffer all [...]
transformed a cart into a makeshift rack and tortured him [...]
part of a night. A female companion of the soldiers ga[...]
chance to escape, but he refused to leave. The next day th[...]
him from a beam by his hands. When they tired of abus[...]
offered him some meat that had been sacrificed to the [...]
meat," said Sabas, "is as impure and profane as Atharidus [...]

An infuriated soldier thrust his javelin at Sabas's ch[...]
thought that he must be dead, but the young man was not [...]
jeered his attacker. "Did you think you killed me? Your jave[...]
as a skein of wool!" Although Sabas was spared once again [...]
lous reprieve, he would not be denied his chance at marty[...]

When word of these events reached Atharidus, he sen[...]
to death by drowning. At the riverside, one of the officials [...]
the execution proposed that they let the young man go. "S[...]
cent," he said, "and Atharidus need never know."

But Sabas rebuked the man and urged him to follow orde[...]
what you cannot see," said the saint. "I see people on the [...]
of the river who are ready to receive my soul and conduct [...]
They are only waiting for the moment when it leaves my bo[...]

The executioners then rigged a plank over Sabas's should[...]
him under water with the board until he drowned.

Witnesses to such a death must have pondered two [...]
"Why?" and "What?" Why had Sabas suppressed his natur[...]
instinct? Why would anyone choose to die? What made Sabas [...]
was in it for him? In their puzzlement, perhaps they thought [...]
life because he was convinced he was going to a better plac[...]

y have perceived that Sabas died because he believed in something
rth more than life itself. But they wouldn't have begun to penetrate
: mystery of this man's death until they posed the most important ques-
n of all: Who? *Who* had so captivated Sabas's heart that he was will-
; to be murdered for his sake? The answer, of course, is Christ—the
e who was murdered for Sabas's sake.

Like Saint Sabas, Saint Apphian was killed by drowning. However,
death was more dramatic because of the miracle that it occasioned.

Apphian was a twenty-year-old youth who lived at Caesarea in the
me of Eusebius, the historian. In his book *The Martyrs of Palestine*,
sebius gave a firsthand account of Apphian's courageous martyrdom
d of a miracle that occurred at his death.

In 303, the emperor Galerius launched a general persecution of
ristians by decreeing that everyone must participate in public sacri-
es. Apphian, his youthful idealism enhanced by his faith, decided to
pose the local enforcement of the decree. Eusebius says the young man
nfided his plan to no one, "not even to us."

Apphian sneaked past the guards to the spot where Urban, the gov-
nor of Caesarea, was offering the sacrifice. He restrained the governor
grabbing his arm. "We must not do this!" he shouted to the crowd.
Vorshiping these lifeless gods is wicked! It will be our doom!"

Eusebius reported that the guards seized Apphian and beat him until
s face was unrecognizable. Then they locked his feet in stocks and con-
ied him to a dungeon. Twenty-four hours later the guards brought the
ung man out and tortured him. They tore his sides, exposing his bones
d entrails, but the brave youth persevered. When asked a question,
e young man simply replied, "I am a servant of Christ!"

The soldiers lighted oil-soaked pieces of flax and held them to his
et. Apphian did not falter even when the fire burnt his flesh to the

bone. His torturers promised relief only if he would offer the pagan sacrifice. "I confess Christ," he said, "the one God, and the same God with the Father." Because Apphian resolutely refused to comply, the magistrate ordered that he be drowned, a sentence the frustrated guards were delighted to carry out. They weighted down Apphian's feet with heavy stones, and with derisive laughter and triumphant shouts they cast him into the sea.

Eusebius says that the entire population witnessed the miracle that occurred upon the young saint's death. A violent earthquake shook both the city and the sea. Then, stones and all, the body of the martyr was hurled out of the water and onto the shore.

The youth's fearless death and the subsequent miracle must have made the people of Caesarea think twice about what they had done.

His witness gives me some second thoughts, too. Apphian loved God so passionately that he adamantly refused to accommodate himself to anything he saw as evil. Nothing, not even the fear of death, could move him to betray the one he loved above all. Apphian's radicalism challenges my mediocrity and makes me ask dangerous questions. Like, how passionately do I love God? What are my true priorities? Does material comfort mean more to me than spiritual reality? Would a little pain or humiliation be enough to swerve me off course? Do I accommodate evil because I am afraid of the consequences? I'd better watch out. Questions like these cut deep.

ᏰᎾᎾᎯᎤ

Being on Purpose

Put Christ first, because he put us first, and let nothing deter us from loving him.

—Saint Cyprian of Carthage

MIRACLES IN HIS MOUTH

Saint Anthony of Padua (1195 — 1231)

*Society, wounded with the sores of evil, is Lazarus. We are the dogs
who must draw near to cure with our tongues—our preaching—
by which we lick with the milk and honey of kindness and gentleness,
healing not aggravating the evils that afflict humankind.*
—SAINT ANTHONY OF PADUA

Had you passed Anthony of Padua on the street, you might not have noticed him. If you had, you would not have been impressed. Short, swarthy, and pudgy, he was quiet and reserved—hardly the life of any party.

Had you heard him preach, however, he would have mesmerized you. His sonorous voice would have captured and held you fast. Like many others in the crowd, you would have been certain he was speaking directly to you. His message might have made you angry. You might have brushed away tears of remorse or felt compelled to action. Whatever your response, you would never have forgotten this Anthony of Padua.

He was a dynamic speaker encased in a reticent person. That is not as paradoxical as it might seem. Anthony's reserve was a shell for a core of strength, and fortitude was his outstanding quality. He was fearless in confronting crowds or individuals, even exalted ones such as princes or bishops. Anthony's character was just the right container for his remarkable charisma, and his preaching was a divine endowment, a supernatural gift.

Saint Anthony had signs and wonders in his preacher's portfolio. But his most significant miracles were subtle, invisible ones that changed peoples' lives. "Preaching," said Anthony, "is a pen which should write faith and virtue in the hearts of the hearers."

Born in Lisbon, Portugal, in 1195, the saint spent his adult life working in Italy and France. His given name was Ferdinand de Bulhões, but he took the name "Anthony" when he entered the Friars Minor, the religious order started by Saint Francis of Assisi. Eventually, he became known as Anthony of Padua because he spent his last five years in that Italian city.

Young Ferdinand was serious, studious, and spiritual. His parents entrusted his early schooling to the priests at the Lisbon cathedral. In 1210, at the age of fifteen, Ferdinand entered the regular canons of Saint Augustine, who had a monastery just outside the city. Because rowdy friends pestered him with frequent visits, Ferdinand was transferred to a house at Coïmbra two years later. There he spent eight quiet years of prayer and study. With his prodigious memory he acquired an extensive knowledge of Scripture, which he would use later in his preaching.

In 1220, the remains of five Franciscans who were martyred in Morocco were brought to Coïmbra. The event fired Ferdinand's desire to give his life for Christ. Since the Augustinian community provided no opportunity for dangerous mission work, he decided to make a change.

The next year he joined the Friars Minor on condition that he would be sent to serve in Morocco. When he left Coïmbra, one of the brothers bid him a teasing farewell: "Well, off you go, since you are so set on becoming a saint!"

"When you hear *me* called a saint," Ferdinand replied, "kneel down and thank God!"

When the new Franciscan—now called Anthony—arrived in Morocco in 1221, he became deathly ill. After only a few months, he was forced to return to Europe. He arrived in Italy just in time for the general meeting of the Friars Minor in Assisi. Saint Francis himself was there, and Anthony felt honored to be in the founder's presence. His reticence hid his abilities from the superiors at the meeting, however, and they deployed him to the obscure hermitage of Saint Paul near Forli. He happily served there with the other brothers, mainly by working in the kitchen.

But the saint was discovered when Dominican and Franciscan friars attended an ordination at Forli. Customarily someone preached at such events, but on this occasion no one was prepared. So the group called on Anthony to speak whatever the Holy Spirit inspired. He begged to be let off, but the group insisted. Reluctantly, Anthony addressed the assembly. He began simply but soon overflowed with intricate reflections based on Scripture and the early Christian writers. Even though the brothers had eaten a hearty meal, no one dozed. They were astounded by the dishwasher's eloquence, passion, and wisdom. Informed of the friar whose real talents were buried at Forli, the regional superior reassigned Anthony to preach throughout northern Italy.

Wherever Anthony went, crowds jammed churches to hear him preach. Often the buildings were too small to hold all those who gathered, so he spoke to thousands in city squares. Many of his hearers decided on the spot to reform their lives, including heretics who had come to watch the show. Spiritual revival occurred wherever he spoke.

The Friars Minor couldn't help but notice Anthony's success. Though his brand of preaching was novel to them, they soon saw its value. Saint Francis of Assisi's simple style of proclaiming the Gospel, along with spontaneous stories and his own dramatic example, had produced the first wave of renewal. Now the community's leaders recognized that Anthony's approach, combining oratory and learning with a charismatic gift, would generate a second one. The order wanted to train others to follow in his footsteps. In 1223, Francis himself appointed Anthony to teach theology to the friars. This was a first. Before this, Francis was wary of study because he feared scholarship might replace devotion in his brothers' hearts.

Of course, the supernatural elements of Saint Anthony's ministry were not reproducible, except by divine intervention. In fact, so many signs and wonders confirmed the saint's words that he is remembered as a miracle worker.

Perhaps Anthony's most famous miracle occurred when he preached to an audience of fish. As he addressed a rambunctious group of heretics who were heckling him, he became discouraged by their unwillingness to listen. He turned to the water nearby. "O fish," he said, "come and hear the word of God." Reportedly, he exhorted the fish to thankfulness for all God's gifts, among them "fins to swim where you will" and the privilege of being Christ's food before and after his resurrection. It is said that hundreds of fish gathered and listened attentively, heads above water, until he dismissed them with a blessing. Then some of the onlookers, touched by the miracle, rejected their errors and returned to the faith.

Once the whole city of Limoges shut down to hear him. Shops closed, and all business ceased. More than thirty thousand people assembled, too many even for the city square, and Anthony led them to an old Roman amphitheater. Just as he began to preach, the sky darkened, pregnant with a violent storm. People made a move to scatter, but the saint stopped them. "Friends, don't leave," he said. "Have confidence in God. I assure you in his name that he will not let one of you get wet." No one moved, and not a drop of rain fell in the theater. When the crowd filed out, however, they discovered that the surrounding area was flooded and covered with large hailstones.

Prophecy was another of Anthony's gifts. An official known for corruption once accosted him in the streets of Le Puy. Every day Anthony had politely bowed to the man, who thought the saint was mocking him. "If I did not fear God's anger," the official said, "I would spit you on my sword!"

"I once hoped for martyrdom," said Anthony, "but I was not worthy of it. But God has shown me that you will become a martyr. When that day comes, remember me and pray for me."

The official laughed in Anthony's face. Not long afterward, however, he had a change of heart. He sold his possessions, gave the money to the poor, and went on pilgrimage with his bishop to Jerusalem. There he vigorously argued issues of faith with a group of Saracens. They seized him, tortured him over three days, and on the fourth day led him out to be executed. On his way to his death, the man remembered Anthony's words and told bystanders that the saint had predicted his unlikely martyrdom.

In November 1225, Anthony preached in Brouges at a synod of two hundred bishops. All present were stunned when he railed at the archbishop, Simon de Sully, who was presiding. "You there, with the miter, I'm talking to you!" he roared. He publicly reprimanded the archbishop for certain secret sins. Deeply moved, the prelate openly wept in repentance, and afterward confided his weakness to Anthony. From that time, de Sully seemed to have experienced renewed zeal, vindicating himself with good behavior for the rest of his life.

Anthony customarily prayed late into the night. Several hosts, curious about their famous guest, spied on him at those times. They claim to have seen Anthony holding a beautiful child and conversing with him. Word got out that Christ came as a child and spoke with the saint, a scene that artists have fixed in the popular mind. They have typically depicted Saint Anthony with the Christ Child standing on an open book. Why do you suppose Christ would choose to come to Anthony not as an adult but as a little child? The place and time of the apparitions may offer a clue. Anthony was ministering in southern France, the home base of the Albigensians, who vigorously denied that Jesus was a human being. What better way for Christ to refute them than to appear as a human child?

To this day, many people ask Saint Anthony's intercession to help them find something they have lost. Perhaps the custom has its roots in the following miracle. A Franciscan novice at the Montpellier house, where Anthony lived, decided to abandon the order. As he left the house, he took one of the saint's valuable manuscripts, a glossary on the Psalms. The youth probably hoped to sell it in order to pay for his flight. When Anthony missed the text, he prayed for its return. It wasn't long before the novice, pale with fear, ran back into the house. Repentant, he returned the book and confessed his wrongdoing to Anthony. He claimed a monstrous image blocked his passage on a bridge and threatened mayhem if he did not return the glossary. The saint forgave the young man, who reconsidered and remained with the friars.

My favorite of all Anthony's wonders was a simple, loving gesture. Pierre, another novice at Limoges, struggled once with temptations to leave the community. Anthony was the superior of the house at the time.

One crisp evening he encountered the young man walking on the monastery grounds. Driven by a profound sense of loneliness, that night the novice was close to deciding that he could no longer stay with the friars. The saint greeted the youth with only his eyes, seeming to look right into his anguished soul. Pierre certainly felt Anthony's love, and it must have seemed like a light in his darkness. Without asking any questions, Anthony gently placed his hands on the novice's shoulders and breathed into his mouth. "Receive the Holy Spirit, Pierre," he said. Miraculously, the young man experienced a dramatic change of heart. Pierre lived to a ripe old age as a Franciscan and loved to repeat that story.

For the last five years of his life, Anthony lived in Padua. His ministry there stirred a great spiritual renewal and a general reform of conduct. He personally settled quarrels, arranged for the release of prisoners, and had people make restitution. He denounced the practice of usury and influenced the passage of laws that reformed the penalties for debtors. He died there in 1231.

"The ideal preacher," Anthony once wrote, "should be hard as flint. From him must spring the spark that gives light to the soul and enkindles in it the fire of divine love." That's a prescription for life-changing miracles. Anthony had described himself to a T.

⌘

The Freedom of Poverty

Poverty is an easy way to God.

Poverty is the mother of humility. It is as difficult to preserve humility amid riches as purity in the midst of delights and luxury.

Poverty sets free. When a person delights in and gloats over his possessions, in reality he limits, even loses his freedom. The mania of riches has enslaved him. He is lowered in status, being no longer the owner but the owned. He has subordinated himself to his goods.

Such servile subjection becomes evident in the fever that dominates him and the anguish that racks him when he loses some of his possessions. In short, true liberty is not found except in voluntary poverty.

Poverty is true riches. So precious is poverty that God's Only-Begotten Son came on earth in search of it. In heaven he had superabundance of all goods. Nothing was lacking there but poverty.

—SAINT ANTHONY OF PADUA

THE MIRACLE IS THE MESSAGE

Saint Vincent Ferrer (1350—1419)

We must see Vincent Ferrer as having one foot in heaven.
—HENRI GHÉON

Saint Vincent Ferrer was a bona fide wonder-worker. Believe it or not, he performed his first miracle when he was still in the womb. A blind woman pressed her head against his mother's stomach and was instantly healed. Once asked how many miracles he had worked, Vincent modestly estimated three thousand. Eight hundred seventy-three of these were carefully documented by the church when it declared him a saint. You can't write long about Vincent Ferrer without mentioning wonders. His life was punctuated with them.

As a child in Valencia, his home town in Aragon, Vincent Ferrer was recognized for his superior spiritual and intellectual gifts. In 1357, when he was just seven years old, his devout parents dedicated him to the service of the church. Eleven years later, he became a member of the

Friars Preachers, the religious order founded by Saint Dominic. He was ordained a priest in 1378. At age twenty-eight, the young saint was already renowned as a theologian, teacher, preacher, and miracle worker.

Vincent's prodigies began to flow in full force in 1374 while he studied at Barcelona. Aragon's harvests were bad that year, and as a result, famine and disease were rampant. Vincent advised the townspeople to beg God's mercy. One Sunday twenty thousand people marched to the city square, where Vincent called them to repentance. At the climax of his sermon he prophesied that relief would come that day: "Have confidence, rejoice in God," he declared, "before night two ships laden with grain will make port."

Few people believed him. Many were furious with disbelief because the weather was so bad it seemed unlikely any ships would reach the harbor. Also annoyed with Vincent's forecast was his superior, who forbade him to exercise his spiritual gifts without permission. That night, however, two supply ships arrived in Barcelona, and Vincent became an instant hero.

Saint Vincent Ferrer's most famous miracle occurred while he was under orders not to use his extraordinary powers. One day as he passed a construction site, a brickworker began to fall from the top of a building. "Brother Vincent," he cried out, "save me!"

"Stay where you are," shouted Vincent, "until I come back." According to eyewitnesses, the brickworker stopped, suspended in midair, while Vincent ran to get his superior's permission to perform a miracle.

"He's waiting?" asked the incredulous superior, stunned by Vincent's request.

"Yes," said Vincent.

"Well, go back and finish it off," said the exasperated superior. Vincent raced back to the hovering man.

"My superior says you may come down," said Vincent, and the man floated safely to the ground.

Such preternatural phenomena did not push Vincent's head into the clouds. Instead, he was preoccupied with compassion for human beings. A friend to the rich and poor alike, he counseled those with grievous personal problems, taught penitents how to live good lives, and settled family quarrels. The preacher and prophet was also a man of public affairs, advising both princes and popes. If Vincent had one foot in heaven, he had planted the other firmly on earth.

The Great Western Schism had started the year Vincent was ordained. Rivals in Rome and Avignon claimed to be pope. For nearly forty years the scandal rent Christendom, afflicting many with faith-diminishing confusion. Vincent was loyal to Clement VII, the Avignon pope. He was also friend, confidant, and confessor to Clement's successor, Benedict XIII, who was elected in 1394.

Vincent consistently pressured Benedict XIII to cooperate with efforts to restore unity, but Benedict obstinately hindered every initiative. The tension of conflicting loyalties to friend and church finally eroded Vincent's health. Afflicted by the stress, he fell seriously ill in 1398.

While Vincent lay near death with fever, Jesus appeared to him. In the vision, the great preachers Dominic and Francis also came to comfort him. Jesus touched Vincent tenderly on the cheek, commanding him to get up. "You will go through the world, preaching," Jesus said, and at that Vincent arose, completely well. It is said that Jesus left permanent finger marks on the saint's face.

Vincent took Jesus' words as a commission for the rest of his life. Armed with ecclesial authority to preach anywhere, he began his international mission in 1399. For the better part of twenty years he journeyed four times through Spain, northern Italy, the Alpine countries, southern Germany, and France. He traveled on foot until an ulcerous leg forced him to ride a donkey.

Whenever Vincent approached a village, people brought their sick so that he might cure them. Thousands of times he raised his hand-held cross as a sign of healing. A dying baby recovers and laughs. An elderly cripple tosses his crutches and dances. A blind girl brushes against him and can see. Miraculous healings in every town, hundreds of times over.

Vincent preached nearly every day, and everywhere he went, thousands gathered to listen to him. His words were touched with a miracle, for even when he couldn't speak the language, everyone in the crowds heard him plainly in their own language, no matter how far they stood from him.

Vincent's main themes were the folly of sin, the necessity of penance, and the imminence of the coming judgment. Like many saints before him, he believed that Jesus would come soon to wrap up human history. Referring to Revelation 14:6, he identified himself as the "angel of the judgment." Though he did not profess to be an angel in human form, he saw himself as Christ's messenger, bearing good news for the repentant and bad news for the hard-hearted.

Once while preaching in Salamanca, he demonstrated his claim with an extraordinary wonder. He commanded some gravediggers in the crowd to bring forward the body of a recently deceased woman.

"Dead woman," he reportedly shouted, "tell these people whether I am the Messenger of the Apocalypse sent to preach the coming of the Last Day."

The woman sat up and said, "Yes, Father, you are that messenger." Then she immediately fell back into her coffin, again a lifeless corpse.

All over Europe people responded to Vincent's preaching with tearful enthusiasm. Many reformed their lives. Multitudes numbering as many as three thousand followed the saint from town to town. Among these was a small group who performed public penance by scourging themselves. To prevent any hint of evil, Vincent organized these penitents into a community that he closely governed. To his credit, in two decades no abuses marred his crusade.

By 1414, three rivals claimed to be pope. That year a council of bishops at Constance deposed one pretender, asked the other two to resign, and arranged for a new election. Benedict XIII brushed off Vincent's appeal that he step down. Because Benedict stubbornly blocked unity that was vital to the church, Vincent urged his vast international following to withdraw their allegiance. With two claimants gone and Benedict isolated, a new pope was chosen and the schism was over. Vincent spent his last years in Brittany and Normandy and died in 1419.

I confess that I did not like Vincent Ferrer much before I studied him. From what I knew, he seemed severe, arrogant, and, yes, a little weird. I soon discovered how mistaken I was. Vincent Ferrer was gentle, humble, and wise. As I watched him move with deft grace through the tormented fourteenth century, I began to admire and even to like him. His anguished times cried out for a saint like him. Vincent lived through the violence of the Hundred Years' War, the malevolence of the bubonic plague, and the turmoil of the Great Schism. Our own century has its share of turbulence—a hundred years of war, the new treacherous plague of AIDS, and shameful racial and religious divisions.

Where are our Saint Vincent Ferrers? We desperately need them.

꩜

The Divine Light Within

You must open the interior eyes of your soul on the light, on this heaven within you, a vast horizon stretching far beyond the realm of human activity, an unexplored country to the majority of human beings. The ordinary observer sees in the ocean only the realm of storms and never guesses that a few feet below the surface its waters are always limpid, and in a scintillating clarity is found vegetation and living creatures of wondrous diversity, marvelous in beauty and structure, mysterious depths where the pearl is formed.

Such is the depth of the soul where God dwells and shows himself to us. And when the soul has seen God, what more can it want? If it possesses him, why and for whom can it ever be moved to abandon him?

So at any price, preserve yourself in that calm through which the soul sees the eternal Sun.

—SAINT VINCENT FERRER

Part Four

∽

Miracles to
Awaken Us

*"Wake up, O sleeper,
rise from the dead,
and Christ will shine on you."*

*Be very careful, then, how you
live—not as unwise but as wise,
making the most of every opportunity, because the days are evil.*

—EPHESIANS 5:14–16

Teresa of Avila claimed that spiritually she was a late bloomer. It was sometime after her fortieth birthday, she said, that her soul experienced an awakening. We should take comfort in the assurance of this great saint's example—it's never too late to get serious about God. We're never too old or too set in our ways to be touched by the supernatural.

What's true for the individual Christian is true for all Christians. From earliest times the church itself has needed spiritual awakening. If you doubt it, just dip into Saint Paul's letters. Try 1 Corinthians, where Paul felt obliged to correct evil practices that had crept into the community. Or why do you suppose he addressed another New Testament church as "you foolish Galatians"?

That the church often needs to be shaken and aroused to spiritual realities should come as no surprise. God seems to have set it up that way. He created the church as a partnership between himself and human beings. Sometimes I wonder why God decided to tie himself to a bunch of sinners. "Didn't you realize," I want to ask him, "how badly we would mess things up?" Then I stop myself, realizing that he knew exactly what he was doing. He desired for the community of believers to have to rely entirely on him.

Look back to the sixteenth century. The church was at its nadir. Spiritual decadence had benumbed it, and political turmoil had wrenched it apart. Yet, in darkness that seemed too thick to dispel, bright lights of renewal began to shine. Saint Francis of Paola stirred the Italian church with throbbing new life. His stupendous miracles were the talk of the whole peninsula. With singular wisdom and integrity, he brought people back to God on their knees.

A short time later, Teresa of Avila spearheaded a spiritual awakening in Spain. She was a most practical mystic, a charming and savvy saint. Teresa was blessed with a diversity of gifts—contemplation, miracles, politics, and pastoral care. And she employed them all strategically to revivify faith throughout Spain.

In the nineteenth century, John Bosco's apostolate to rescue homeless boys sparked a renewal throughout northern Italy. Against odds that would stop most of us, the saint evangelized and cared for thousands of desperate young men. From these castouts he recruited and formed a new religious order that would have a profound influence on the rest of the church. He did it all with nothing but faith in his arsenal. When he turned to God for aid, God didn't disappoint him. Every day of John Bosco's life was strewn with visions, revelations, signs, and miracles.

And what about Francis of Assisi? He launched a movement that brought spiritual reformation to all of thirteenth-century Europe. His tiny, ragtag band of followers miraculously multiplied into thousands in a few short years. Seven hundred years later, the church still draws refreshment from his radical decision to follow Christ.

Two compelling facts stand out from the example of these four saints. First, spiritual awakening emerges neither from clever programs nor detailed strategies, but, rather, it comes one heart at a time. Second, God sometimes chooses to bring spiritual replenishment to millions through one person's life of faith.

None of these saints set out to found religious communities. None had planned to spawn renewals or to reform the church. Their aims were more personal. They simply wanted to love God above anything else— a goal we would be wise to make our own.

გოთთ

MIRACLES FOR THE POOR
Saint Francis of Assisi (1181–1226)

☙ ❧

*You will never understand Francis till you realize that with
all the love and loyalty of his heart he married Poverty for
Christ's sake. She was the Princess Poverty.*
—C. C. MARTINDALE, S. J.

The people of Assisi thought Francis was crazy.

Francis gave them plenty of evidence for their view. What would *you* say about a rich kid who seemed to change overnight from partygoer to ascetic? Who swapped his fine clothes for a beggar's rags, gleefully renounced his inheritance, and stripped naked in a bishop's court? Who kissed lepers, preached to birds, and claimed that Jesus spoke to him from a crucifix?

Had I personally observed Francis's unusual behavior, I think I might have agreed with his critics. "Of course I favor taking Christianity seriously," I might have said, "but Francis has gone too far." No doubt I would have echoed the voice of reason, warning of extremism and praising balance.

Francis certainly was an extremist. But weren't all the saints? While it's true that he was unbalanced, in the sense that he did not limit his enthusiasm, Francis was anything but insane. To the contrary, you could argue that he had a healthier mind than most of us. Unlike him, we focus narrowly on the material world. We wear blinders that shut out the broader and deeper spiritual realm. By so doing, we place ourselves out of touch with a vast part of reality. So perhaps we are the ones who are a little "crazy" or "insane."

Francis's view was spiritually panoramic. When he observed the ordinary, he perceived it with a breadth and depth we often miss. He looked beyond the human to behold the divine.

Born in Assisi in 1181, Francis was the son of Peter Bernardone, a successful merchant, who thought the world of his son. As a youth, he was infatuated with the romantic world of chivalry and sometimes imagined himself an armored knight. He dreamed of fame and glory and was not much interested either in formal education or in his father's business. With plenty of money, he preferred to organize parties for the town's young people. Though never a profligate, he enjoyed his role as leader of the revelers. Even so, he gave generously to the poor.

Francis's conversion occurred more gradually than is usually thought. During a civil war in 1201, he was captured and imprisoned in Perugia. After a year he was released, only to be afflicted with a serious illness. Characteristically, he bore both his imprisonment and the disease with cheerful patience, though afterward he was more serene and serious.

On his recovery, he decided to join the war effort in southern Italy. He outfitted himself lavishly in hopes of joining the army of Duke Walter III of Brienne. One day, however, he met a poor man in shabby clothes. Overcome by compassion, the would-be warrior traded his expensive suit for the beggar's rags.

That same night, Francis had a prophetic dream, which at first he misunderstood. He envisioned a great castle packed with armaments bearing the sign of the cross. He thought he heard a voice say that the weapons were for him and his soldiers. He also sensed that a lovely bride awaited him there. True enough, but Francis did not yet understand that these would be spiritual warriors and his a spiritual bride.

Encouraged by this vision, Francis set out to join the Duke's army. He never arrived. He took ill again en route. On his sickbed he heard a divine voice ask, "Which is better? To serve the servant or the Lord?"

"Of course, to serve the Lord," Francis answered.

"Then why make a master of the servant?"

Francis began to get the idea. When he returned to Assisi, he resumed his former pattern of life, but he had lost his enthusiasm for it. His friends noticed that he seemed distracted amid the merriment and suggested that perhaps he had fallen in love. "Yes," said Francis, "I am going to take a wife more beautiful and more worthy than any you know." In the squalor of Assisi's back streets, Francis had caught sight of Lady Poverty. She had captivated him, and he was determined to embrace her.

Francis took some hesitant steps toward her by devoting himself to prayer. He also made a pilgrimage to Rome, where he spent a day as a beggar. The experience revolted him. He returned home still nauseated by the stench and repulsed by the humiliation. He started to give alms publicly, right from his own door. However, these charitable acts made him feel condescending and paternalistic. Instead of looking down on the poor, he wanted to look up to them.

One day, while riding on the Assisi plain, Francis gave alms to a leper. It was a decisive step. As Francis offered his gift, he suppressed his disgust and kissed the leper's hand. In turn, the leper lifted his face and gave Francis the kiss of peace. At that, something broke deep inside of Francis.

A miracle expedited Francis's conversion, one that set the course of his life. One day he was praying in the church of Saint Damian, on the outskirts of Assisi. Suddenly a voice from a crucifix said to him three times, "Francis, go and repair my house, which you see is falling down." Francis shook with terror, and at that moment he was profoundly changed. Thomas of Celano, Francis's first biographer, saw in this event the source of the saint's unwavering devotion to the crucified Christ.

Francis thought that God had told him to repair the church of Saint Damian, which was literally collapsing. In a misguided moment, he sold some of his father's merchandise and offered the money to the priest at Saint Damian. Terrified of Francis's belligerent father, the priest prudently declined the gift, and the saint left it on a windowsill.

When he discovered what Francis had done, Peter Bernardone was hurt and enraged. He beat his son mercilessly and locked him up in chains. Then he dragged Francis before Bishop Guido of Assisi to settle the issue. Bernardone then issued an ultimatum. Francis could pay for the goods he had taken and return home, or else he could forfeit his inheritance. At the bishop's direction, Francis agreed to pay for the merchandise. Then he renounced his inheritance with a dramatic gesture. "The clothes I wear are also his," Francis declared. "I will give them back." With that, he stripped off all of his clothes. Then he turned to his father. "Up till now I have called you father on earth," he said. "From now on I say, 'Our Father, who art in heaven.'"

For several years Francis roamed the roads of central Italy, shabbily dressed and carrying a pilgrim's staff. He returned to Assisi to beg money to complete the reconstruction of the Saint Damian church. Similarly, he arranged for the repair of Saint Mary of the Angels, nicknamed the Portiuncula, or "little piece."

At this church in 1209 Francis was first shown the life pattern that he and his disciples would follow. One day at Mass, a particular Scripture passage, Matthew 10:7–10, struck him profoundly. "As you go, preach this message: 'The kingdom of heaven is near.' Heal the sick, raise the dead, cleanse those who have leprosy, drive out demons. Freely you have received, freely give. Do not take along any gold or silver or copper in your belts; take no bag for the journey, or extra tunic, or sandals or a staff." Francis took these words as God's personal direction to him.

On the spot, he embraced this gospel ideal. Francis shed his extra clothes and his shoes, keeping only a coat that he tied about himself with a cord. He went from town to town, urging everyone to repent. Everywhere, people were deeply moved at his words. He charmed his hearers by presenting the demands of the Gospel in the romantic language of the troubadours. He would later implement the commands to heal and set people free.

During these years Francis accumulated a band of followers. By 1210, a dozen men had embraced the saint's ideals. They wore habits of undyed woolen coats tied with cords, the dress of poor peasants. Francis offered them a simple life consisting of the requirements of the Gospel. He called his brothers "Friars Minor." They were to be "lesser" because he wanted them to take the low position of servants. That year, Francis went to Rome to seek approval for his community from Pope Innocent III. Prompted by a vision of Francis holding up a falling church building, the pope gave verbal consent and commissioned the Friars Minor to preach repentance.

When Francis was rebuilding Saint Damian's, he had often prophesied that someday it would be a convent. "Help me finish this building," he said. "Here one day will be a monastery of nuns who will bring glory to the Lord throughout the church." Now, years later in 1212, Clare of

Assisi joined Francis, starting a community of women committed to his life pattern. Francis's prophecy about Saint Damian came true when she and her sisters took up residence there.

Preaching Christ crucified and loving him in the poor dominated Francis's attention. It was the heart of his ministry. Miracles, visions, and prophecies occurred plentifully, but they were only side effects. He barely noticed them. Here is just a sampler:

Once in Spoleto, a man with a cancerous face met Saint Francis. Hideously malformed, the man tried to throw himself at the saint's feet. Francis, however, stopped him. He took the man's diseased face in his hands and kissed him on both cheeks. On the spot, the man was completely healed of all disfigurement. "I don't know which I ought to wonder at most," said Saint Bonaventure, a later follower of Saint Francis, "such a kiss or such a cure."

At Toscanella, Francis was housed with a soldier's family. The man's small son was crippled and confined to an infant's cradle. Completely immobile, the little boy had never even crawled. At first, Francis refused the soldier's requests to heal his child, because the saint felt he was unworthy of such great grace. But finally he prayed, laid his hand on the boy, and blessed him. Then Francis lifted the child from his crib and set him on his feet. Healed, the lad showed his new strength by walking—probably strutting quite proudly—all about the house.

One day in Gubbio, a lady with severely deformed hands ran up to Francis. "Just touch them," she pleaded, and raised her misshapen hands to the saint. Francis clasped her hands in his, gently moved his fingers over hers, and she was healed on the spot. What do you think she did next? What any Italian woman would do. She used her restored hands to cook. She went off and baked a cheesecake for Saint Francis. He ate some of it and sent the rest back for her family.

Everyone knows that wild creatures of every sort miraculously became tame in Francis's presence. Thomas of Celano tells of the rabbit and the pheasant who could not bear to be separated from him; the friendly falcon who awakened Francis at night for prayer but did not do so when the saint was sick; the cricket who would rest in his hand and sing at Francis's request; and many others. Thus, Francis is honored as patron saint of animal lovers.

Francis especially liked birds, and a popular account tells how he once preached to them. However, Francis liked birds in more ways than one, as the following story shows. Once, while traveling through Spain, Francis became sick. While recovering, he confessed to his companion that he would very much like to eat a bird, if he had one. At that, a man on horseback rode up and gave Francis a fine fowl, already prepared for cooking. Francis received the gift with relish and soon enjoyed his impromptu barbecue. I particularly like this anecdote because it peels the romantic veneer from Saint Francis by showing his humanity, a side of him we rarely see.

Once in the early days, Francis had prophesied to a few friars that a great number of men would join them. He also foretold that the Friars Minor would spread throughout the world. By the general meeting of the order in 1221, his words had come true. Friaries were established in Italy, Spain, France, Germany, and Hungary. In time, the saint regretted that his community had grown so large. Its size now required an organization that favored owning property and thus threatened Lady Poverty. However, in 1223, Pope Honorius III officially approved a rule for the Friars Minor that embodied Francis's ideals. Controversy over worldly concerns such as possessions, however, seethed in the order and eventually divided it.

In 1224, Francis retired with only one companion to a tiny hermitage on Mount Alvernia. Here an extraordinary miracle occurred. One day in a vision Francis saw a great seraph, a high-ranking angel, who was nailed to a cross. As the saint beheld this apparition, nail marks appeared in his own hands and feet. A gaping wound opened on his right side, as if he had been pierced with a lance. This painful, physical replication of Christ's wounds is called the "stigmata," a phenomenon reserved for only a few saints. How are we to understand this mysterious and mystical experience? One way is to view the stigmata as a marvelous sign of Francis's extraordinary intimacy with the crucified Christ.

Francis died in 1226. People had ceased thinking he was crazy long before. Rather, as with Mother Teresa in our day, they welcomed him everywhere as a living saint. In a dozen years, Saint Francis had initiated a movement that would bring new life to the church throughout thirteenth-century Europe. The saint's ability to enchant souls continues. Over the centuries, he has awakened hundreds of thousands of his followers to the light of the Spirit.

⁙

Prayer to Christ Crucified

We adore you, Christ, here and in all your churches which are in the whole world, and we bless you because by your holy cross you have redeemed the world.

—SAINT FRANCIS OF ASSISI

A MIRACLE IN HER SOUL

Saint Teresa of Avila (1515 – 1582)

⌒〰〰〰⌒

Come, Creator, Spirit come
From your bright heavenly throne,
Come, take possession of our souls
And make them all your own. . . . .

O guide our minds with your blest light
With love our hearts inflame. . . . .
——*VENI CREATOR SPIRITUS*

Some devoted students of the saints exalt them too highly. These overzealous hagiographers do the saints a great disservice. They daub their subjects' blemishes with cosmetic religiosity. They seal saints from us in airtight wrappers or isolate them on pedestals. Haven't you read biographies of saints who are made to seem like visitors from other planets? Such well-intentioned writers also do us a great disservice. They put the saints beyond our reach by concealing their humanity.

I find these spiritual giants more attractive when their mortality plainly shows. When, among their wonders, I see their wrongdoings and weaknesses, I can relate to them more easily.

Little danger, however, that any hagiographer, no matter how uncritical or pious, could obscure the humanness of Teresa of Avila. If a biographer attempted to put Teresa on a pedestal, I'm convinced she would hastily climb down. "I didn't like it up there very much," she would say. "From silly devotions and sour-faced saints," she once said, "good Lord deliver us!"

Teresa herself was anything but silly or sour-faced. This splendid woman was graced with heavenly ecstasies but never ceased to enjoy earthly creatures. "I could be bribed with a sardine," she once confessed. Teresa bore her radiance in a clay pot. Her life seemed a perfect blend of the natural and the supernatural, the human and the divine. Once, a visitor was shocked to find the holy woman delightfully devouring a partridge someone had given her. Was this the way of the ascetic? What would people think? "Let them think what they please," said the saint, licking her fingers. "There's a time for partridge and a time for penance." Is it any wonder that Teresa has such universal appeal?

We love Teresa of Avila for her candid self-revelation. She does not tell us about her raptures without also confessing her faults. We admire her intelligent approach to spirituality. Teresa invites us to discipline ourselves in prayer and, in the same breath, casually reminds us to relax and recreate. We appreciate her view that common sense is a prerequisite to the spiritual life. Innocent of sentimentality, she refreshes us. "Even though the Lord should give this young girl devotion," she once wrote, "and teach her contemplation, if she has no sense she never will come to have any, and instead of being of use to the community she will be a burden." Here's one of Teresa's delicious exclamations that failed to make it into any of my saint books. "May God preserve us from stupid nuns!" Oh, to have been able to quote that line when I was in fourth grade!

In 1535, at age twenty, Teresa entered the Carmelite convent of the Incarnation at Avila. By her own admission, over the next twenty years her progress in the spiritual life was spotty and slow. Life was lax at the monastery, where the sisters indulged in a somewhat worldly, free-wheeling social life. Teresa was no exception. She later described herself as quite a "gadabout." But things changed when she turned forty. Inspired moments with Augustine's *Confessions* and a picture of the suffering Christ persuaded Teresa to renew her commitment to serious prayer. At that time she began to receive visions and interior communications from God.

Such spiritual phenomena were controversial in sixteenth-century Spain, as they still are. To determine their genuineness, a spiritual adviser directed Teresa to seek only those things most pleasing to God. He told her to pray daily the *Veni Creator Spiritus*, the ancient invocation of the Holy Spirit.

One day as Teresa prayed that lovely hymn, she was caught up for the first time in ecstasy. She heard within these words, "I will not have you hold conversations with men, but with angels." Thereafter, the trickle of Teresa's mystical experiences swelled to a torrent. One of her visions was a terrifying revelation of the horrors of hell that galvanized her faith and commitment.

Teresa tried her best to keep her divine communications secret, but Avila was a small town, and word got out. For several years, the saint suffered greatly from accusations of hypocrisy and demonism. Finally, however, Saint Peter of Alcantara, a widely respected spiritual director, declared that she was clearly being led by the Spirit.

The great miracle in Saint Teresa's life was not something she did but something that was done to her. As she grew in intimacy with God, she repeatedly experienced an extraordinary palpable sign of their closeness. It was as though God literally took possession of her heart and set it aflame with love.

Following is her own description of the divine invasion of her soul: "I saw an angel close by me, on my left side, in bodily form. He was not large, but small of stature and most beautiful—his face burning, as if he were one of the highest angels, who seem to be all of fire. . . . I saw in his hand a long spear of gold, and at the iron's point there seemed to be a little flame. He appeared to me to be thrusting it at times into my heart, and to pierce my very entrails; when he drew it out, he seemed to draw them out also, and to leave me all on fire with a great love of God."

The popular mind identifies this vision with Saint Teresa. Artists and sculptors have often depicted it, the most famous representation being the seventeenth-century statue by Giovanni Bernini. Saint John of the Cross, Teresa's friend and contemporary, described Teresa's experience as "the cauterization of her soul." He saw it as a profound mystical event reserved for a very few.

Words cannot describe what really happened to the saint. Teresa says that God touched her heart in a delightful yet painful way, leaving her soul afire with love for him. An astonishing fact witnessed to the truth of her words: According to a physician's testimony, after her death, Saint Teresa's heart was found to bear a long, deep scar.

Perhaps the best test of Teresa's mysticism is her activism. Her heaven-sent ecstasies seemed to focus her attention on earthly concerns. She demonstrated her love for God through her service to others. Only two years old when Martin Luther launched the Protestant movement, she became a Catholic reformer in the Age of Reformation. By the time she was an adult, the Reformation was in full swing throughout Europe. Teresa contributed to the Catholic Reformation by awakening the religious ardor of men and women everywhere. Throughout Spain, she established renewed communities that adhered closely to the original Carmelite rule of life.

One September evening in 1560, Teresa and a few friends discussed the unhappy state of affairs at the convent of the Incarnation. They decried the lax observance of the rule, the predominance of cliques, and the excessive involvement with the outside world. Teresa probably expressed her strongly held opinion that too many sisters were jammed together into one place. "Experience has taught me," she said, "what a house full of women is like. God preserve us from such a state." During the conversation, Maria de Campo, Teresa's niece, made a lighthearted suggestion. "We'd probably be better off to start over at a new convent," she said. "Maybe then we could become real followers of the hermits of Mount Carmel."

For Teresa the idea was no joke. Believing that the Holy Spirit was behind her niece's suggestion, she soon had things underway. Before long, she had secured financial backing and permission from the Carmelites and the church. But opposition erupted immediately. First, the people of Avila raised an uproar. The town, they said, could not possibly afford to support another monastery. Then the sisters at the convent of the Incarnation raised their voices in protest. Teresa's plan cut too close to the bone, threatening their comfortable lifestyle. At one time, a priest railed from the pulpit against wandering nuns who tried to start new religious orders. A few heads turned to gape at Teresa, who sat toward the back of church, chuckling quietly. She was laughing because she expected God to act, and he did.

Visions assured Teresa that God wanted her to establish the new community. Behind the scenes, her friends worked to garner official support. Money arrived miraculously just when it was needed. Teresa secretly constructed a small house as her future convent, pretending that the building was a home for the family of her married sister, Juana.

An accident on the construction site occasioned a charming miracle. Juana's little son, Gonzalez, was playing with pieces of stone and was crushed when a wall collapsed on him. Juana howled with anguish when she dug his broken body from the rubble, for, to all appearances, her child was dead. His father rushed the lifeless boy to Teresa, who took him in her arms, lowered her veil, and bent her head close to his. The saint breathed a prayer over her nephew. Instantly, Gonzalez revived, as if waking from sleep, and he began to play with Teresa's face, his little fingers tracing a smile on her lips. A touch of the supernatural had healed the child. Later, Gonzalez often teased his aunt about this incident. "Aunt Teresa," he would say, "you'd better be praying hard for me. It's your fault that I'm not already with God in heaven."

Amid much commotion, Teresa and four sisters opened the convent of Saint Joseph on August 24, 1562. Gradually, opposition died down, and the sisters won the respect of all. Within five years, the Carmelites and the church were encouraging Teresa to establish additional monasteries. King Philip II encouraged the Catholic Reformation and strongly supported the renewal of convents and monasteries. Between 1567 and 1582, Saint Teresa founded seventeen reformed Carmelite convents throughout Spain.

For her sisters, Teresa prescribed a simple life, rigorously based on the primitive Carmelite rule. Given her convictions about size, she allowed only thirteen women in a convent. The sisters lived in poverty, supporting themselves by begging. They spent long periods in silence and solitude and wore uncomfortable habits made from coarse serge. They went without shoes, wearing only sandals, from which the new community got its name—the "Discalced" Carmelites. But Teresa also punctuated the seriousness of convent life with fun. With tambourines, dance, and spontaneous songs, the sisters frequently celebrated Christian feasts and special occasions. Thus, none of her sisters would have a chance to become "sour-faced."

Two little miracles occurred in the early days at Saint Joseph's, that characterize Teresa's wit and work. One involved a plague of lice. The other, a well.

First, the saint's wit. One day the sisters determined to get rid of hordes of lice that had infested their rough clothing. Early in the morning the nuns marched in procession all through the house to the chapel, carrying a cross and singing psalms. They implored God to free them from the parasites. Then Teresa blessed her sisters, their rooms and beds, singing a spontaneous song with this delightful refrain, "Do Thou keep all nasty creatures out of this serge!" Immediately the lice vanished and never plagued the sisters again.

Second, her life's work. Saint Joseph's convent lacked a water supply. In fact, the water on the property was inaccessibly deep and rumored to be undrinkable. Against expert advice, Teresa sank a well, from which fresh, clear water flowed. Today, four hundred years later, Teresa's well still provides water for the convent!

When Teresa was a child, a picture of Jesus speaking with the Samaritan woman at the well hung on a wall in her room. She often stood before it and prayed, "Lord, give me of that water that I may not thirst." Now, quite appropriately, the well at Saint Joseph's is called "Samaritan's Well."

༄

Prayer Cultivates Virtue

The beginner must think of himself as setting out to make a garden in which the Lord is to take his delight, yet in soil most unfruitful and full of weeds. His Majesty uproots the weeds and will set good plants in their stead. We have now, by God's help, like good gardeners, to make these plants grow. We must water them carefully, so that they may not perish, but may produce flowers which shall send forth great fragrance to give refreshment to this Lord of ours, so that he may often come into the garden to take his pleasure and his delight among these virtues.

—SAINT TERESA OF AVILA

RAISING THE DEAD AND OTHER MIRACLES

Saint Francis of Paola (1416—1507)

❧

*Heal the sick, raise the dead, cleanse those who have leprosy,
drive out demons. Freely you have received, freely give. Do not take
along any gold or silver or copper in your belts.*
—MATTHEW 10:8–9

Saint Francis of Paola's miracles were more diverse than those of any other saint we've looked at. He seems to have possessed a comprehensive authority over nature akin to that of Christ himself. When Francis gave a command "in the name of charity," earth, fire, water, disease, and death all seemed to obey. For example, he defied gravity to move huge boulders. He passed through fire and handled glowing coals unharmed. He redirected streams with a word. He healed the blind. He raised the dead. Repeatedly.

This saint was so simple and his miracles so extraordinary that it's easy to miss the significance of his life and work. Focusing on the wonders might give the false impression that he was a show-off or a weirdo. Thus, a little background will help us appreciate him properly.

Francis of Paola founded a community of priests and brothers that he called the Minim, which means the "least." He and his followers imitated the humility and poverty of Francis of Assisi, the saint's namesake. In 1435, Francis started his first monastery in Paola, his hometown in Calabria, located in the heel of the Italian boot. Francis was not formally educated and was never ordained a priest, but he was a gifted evangelist and pastor. His charismatic personality attracted hundreds of followers whom he formed in the spiritual disciplines and built into strong brotherhoods. Before his death, Francis established Minim communities in Italy, Sicily, and France.

When Francis came on the scene, grave dangers were menacing both church and state. At the turn of the sixteenth century, Italy was racked with internecine wars. The city-states were in conflict with the popes, who at the time headed a secular state as well as the church. What was worse, the Turks, who had overrun eastern Europe and the Mediterranean Sea, were threatening to conquer the western countries. At the same time, serious problems plagued the church. Piety was at a low ebb, devotion was distorted, and corruption and neglect were on the rise in the ecclesiastical bureaucracies.

Amid these darkening circumstances, Francis of Paola was a beacon of integrity and holiness. He and his brothers spawned spiritual renewal everywhere they were located, especially in southern Italy. Francis's dynamic gifts and practical wisdom caught the attention of state and church alike. During his lifetime, the saint counseled and confronted five kings and seven popes.

Francis worked many of his earliest miracles during the construction of his first monastery in 1435. One day, a huge boulder sat in the middle of the site. Try as they might, the workmen could not dislodge it. So Francis knelt in prayer, and the gigantic stone popped out of the ground. A flabbergasted construction crew easily rolled it aside. On another day an immense rock began to rumble down a hill toward the workers. "In the name of charity, stop!" shouted Francis, and it stopped dead. He also stretched a beam that was too short, lifted an enormous log the workmen couldn't budge, and provided drinking water by striking the ground with a stick—always "in the name of charity," because Francis thought only of loving others.

Twice he revived fatally injured workers. He once knelt in prayer beside the body of a man crushed by a beam. Francis touched the mangled corpse with some herbs, and the workman got up, as though he had been simply taking a nap. A falling tree killed another laborer named Domenico Sapio. "In the name of charity, Domenico, arise!" commanded Francis. Domenico got up, brushed himself off, thanked Francis, and returned to work as if nothing had happened.

Francis's fame as a wonder-worker quickly spread throughout Calabria. Rich and poor came to him seeking miraculous help. Giacomo di Tarsia, a local baron, came to the monastery with his wife, Giovanna, and retinue of friends and servants. He asked Francis to heal an abscess that doctors had said might require amputation of his leg. Francis sent one of the monks to his vegetable garden to pick some blades of an herb called "horse's toenail." Then Francis went alone to the chapel to pray. When the saint returned, he placed three blades of the herb over the baron's sore, bandaged it, and told him to go home. A few miles down the road from Paola, Giacomo said to his wife, "Giovanna, my leg does not hurt anymore." When the baron removed the wrap, he discovered that the abscess was completely gone. With whoops of laughter, he dismounted from his horse and ran about to show off his healing.

The saint cured the deaf, the mute, and the blind. From birth, Bartolo di Scigliano could neither hear nor speak. The doctors could do nothing for the little boy, and as a last resort his parents brought him to Francis. The saint sat down and stood Bartolo on his knee so that the boy and he would be face-to-face. Francis prayed briefly, then said with a smile, "My son, repeat after me, 'Jesus, Jesus, Jesus.'" During an agonizing moment of silence, the parents feared that nothing had happened. Then, "Jesus!" stammered the boy. The parents gasped with awe as, louder and more clearly, their son spoke. "Jesus!" Finally, shaking with excitement, little Bartolo shouted, "Jesus!" A touch of the supernatural had changed his life forever.

Seventeen-year-old Giulia Catalano was born sightless. Her parents brought her to Francis, who was working in the garden. The saint greeted the family and then turned to Giulia. "Would you like me to ask God to give you your sight?" he asked.

"Oh, yes, Brother Francis, please pray for me," she replied.

Francis blessed an herb he held in his hands and touched it to Giulia's eyes. All watched expectantly. When the saint removed his fingers from the girl's face, she could see. Guilia blinked, and—wide-eyed—looked right at Francis. Her first experience with sight was to look upon the face of the wonder-worker who had healed her.

A young couple's infant son was born without eyes and with a deformed face. Crazed with anger and despair, the parents had nearly given up hope when they heard of the miracle worker in Calabria. The distraught father took his baby to the saint, wondering if Francis could do something for the child. "God loves your son," Francis said. "Don't be afraid. I will pray and ask him to heal the baby." Then he knelt in prayer and raised his arms to heaven. He wet his index finger with saliva and traced eyes on the infant's misshapen face. "In the name of charity," he said, "little brother, open your eyes!" Instantly the baby's eyes appeared, and he looked around in wonder. Dazzled with joy, the boy's father choked up and began to weep with loud, happy sighs. Francis continued to touch the infant's face until normal features replaced all disfigurements. When he was satisfied that the boy's healing was complete, he placed him in his father's arms. A smiling father returned home, bearing a smiling baby.

Word of the Calabrian wonder-worker spread throughout Europe. Pope Paul II, who sought ways to bring spiritual renewal to the church, took an interest in Francis. In 1470, he sent his trusted associate, Father Girolamo Adorno, to investigate the saint's activities. The pope wanted to know more about Francis's miracles, his severe pattern of life, and his growing number of followers and monasteries.

Adorno greeted Francis in church and tried to kiss his hand. The saint politely refused the gesture and startled the papal envoy with a fact he could only have known by revelation. "I should be kissing your hand," said Francis, "which has been consecrated for priestly service for more than thirty years." Later that day, Adorno attempted to persuade Francis to mitigate the severity of his community's pattern of life. The Minims disciplined themselves rigorously, observing a strict lifelong fast and abstaining from meat and dairy products. "You can withstand these rigors because you are a sturdy peasant," said Adorno. "But it isn't wise to impose such austerity on others who might not be able to survive it."

Francis silently walked over to a charcoal fire. With his bare hands he scooped up burning coals and, unharmed, held them before the stunned priest. "Yes, Father," he said, "I am only an unlearned peasant, and if I were not, I would not be able to do this." Adorno did not miss the subtlety of this dramatic reply.

Before the priest returned to Rome, he interviewed many of the people who were miraculously cured. Among them were the Baron Giacomo di Tarsia, whose leg Francis had cured, and Francesco Rocco, the disfigured infant he had healed, who was now a handsome young man.

Impressed by the results of his inquiry, Father Adorno returned to assure the pope of Francis's authenticity. Paul II was pleased but still withheld approval of the Minim because he felt the strict fast endangered the well-being of the monks. But his successor, Pope Sixtus IV, after further investigations, gave blanket approval to the order in 1473.

The mounting Turkish threat to southern Italy alarmed Francis. He spoke urgently of the impending danger, exhorting everyone to prayer and repentance. He prophesied that Otranto, a port at the tip of the peninsula, would fall to the Turks on July 28, 1480. Francis wrote two letters to Ferdinand, King of Naples. The saint urged the king to quit meddling in Italian quarrels and to protect his eastern cities from the Turks. The king ignored Francis, whom he regarded as a religious fanatic. Otranto fell to the Turks on the exact day Francis had designated. That caught the king's attention. He redirected his armies, but it took fourteen months to win the city back.

Francis continued to warn Ferdinand to stop oppressing his people. The saint publicly admonished the king to establish a humane administration. Annoyed by Francis's constant opposition and the opening of new monasteries in Naples, Ferdinand ordered his arrest. The soldiers sent to capture Francis searched the monastery but could not find him. A workman challenged the captain of the troops. "How can it be," he asked, "that you do not see the servant of God? You have passed him many times."

"Where is he then?" demanded the angry captain. The worker led him to the church, where Francis was praying in the sanctuary. He had been invisible to the soldiers, who had searched the church several times.

The captain fell to his knees when he finally saw Francis. "In the name of charity, get up!" said Francis. "Tell the king for me that he is a man of little faith if he believes that my presence would help him. Tell him he had better change his behavior and reform his government or else he and his household will not avoid God's judgment."

Impressed by Francis's miraculous powers and strength of character, the captain persuaded Ferdinand to stop harassing him. But Ferdinand did not change his ways, and the saint's prophetic warning came true. Two decades later, the Spanish conquered Naples and overthrew Ferdinand's descendants.

In 1481, King Louis XI of France was slowly dying in the aftermath of a serious stroke. He asked Saint Francis to come and heal him. At first Francis refused. However, the king appealed to Pope Sixtus IV, and the pope told the saint to go. When Francis arrived, Louis fell on his knees and begged for healing.

"The lives of kings," said Francis, "are in the hands of God and have divinely appointed limits. You should address your prayers to him." Francis had received a revelation that the king would not survive the illness. The king persisted in his requests but without success. Over time Francis's kindness won his confidence, and the two became friends. By the saint's word and example, Louis seems to have reckoned with God. Peacefully accepting his fate, he began regularly to consult Francis on personal and political matters. When the king died, he was resting in the saint's arms.

Francis never returned to Calabria. He remained twenty-five years in the French court, where he became a trusted adviser to the kings of France and a representative of the pope.

In his youth, Francis of Paola once revived his pet lamb, Martinello, after the animal was killed by some local workmen. That was just practice, I suppose. As Francis matured, he became much more than a wonder-worker. I like to think of him as a Christian statesman with marvelous powers, an ambassador for the Gospel who performed miracles as he went about his work.

ᏯᎳᎳᏱ

Farewell Letter

Sons of mine, whom I so love in the charity of Jesus Christ, I am separating myself from you to go to France. Hear the recommendations that I as your father in Jesus Christ leave with you. Love above all else our merciful Father in heaven, and serve him with all your strength and purity of heart.

Maintain and mortify your members with a salutary and discreet penance, which will not permit you to fall victim to the insidious lures of the devil. He cannot triumph except over those who are slothful and negligent. In the trials and temptations we face regularly in our daily lives, help one another.

Obey with humility your superiors, for obedience is the backbone of faith. Be sympathetic to the weaknesses and failings of others. Persevere in your holy vocation, to which the Lord has so obviously called you. Keep in mind that the crown of salvation is won only by those who persevere. It is vain to begin a good action unless you bring it to full completion. Maintain yourselves with holy emulation on the path of virtue which I have so ardently pursued, particularly the practice of charity, humility, and patience.

Good-bye, my priests and brothers. We shall never again see each other on earth! May the Lord unite us in heaven!

—SAINT FRANCIS OF PAOLA TO HIS BROTHERS,
FEBRUARY 1483

MIRACLES, DREAMS, AND VISIONS

Saint John Bosco (1815—1888)

༄

In his life the supernatural almost became the natural,
the extraordinary, the ordinary.
—POPE PIUS XI

I think God may have smiled at the joke he played when he sent Saint John Bosco as a gift to nineteenth-century Europe. The saint was a wonder-worker among people who did not believe in miracles.

Nineteenth-century Europe was a revolutionary era. Kings and kingdoms were overthrown. New nations were forged by war and conquest. Democracies were born. Darwin and Marx spun new ideas that would radically alter the human experience. Emphasis was on the material, the natural, the power of humankind to set its own directions. The supernatural, the church, and even God himself were out of favor with the movers and shakers of the culture.

Saint John Bosco was a sign of contradiction in this age of unbelief. During his lifework of caring for homeless boys, he performed thousands of miracles. They seemed to slip out of him. Hardly a day passed without his precipitating some supernatural intervention—a revelation, a prophecy, a mysterious appearance, a multiplication of food, a healing. So numerous and extraordinary were John Bosco's miracles that one of his biographers described his life as "an astonishing invasion of the supernatural."

The saint experienced a life-shaping dream in 1824, when he was only nine years old. He saw himself in a field, surrounded by children who were yelling and fighting. He tried to calm them, first by persuasion, then by force. "Don't use violence," said a mysterious person. "Be gentle if you want to win their friendship." The children had momentarily transmogrified into wild animals, but now they appeared to become submissive lambs. Then, rising above the scene, a woman's voice instructed John to "Take your crook and lead them out to pasture." That dream set the course of the saint's life, and it recurred to lead him at crucial junctions of his life.

From his youth, John Bosco was consumed by a passionate concern to rescue homeless boys. As a young man, he made sporadic efforts to reach out to young men in his neighborhood. His real ministry, however, began in 1841, when he was ordained a priest at Turin, in northern Italy. There, he began by gathering boys on Sundays for informal days of recreation and teaching. Gradually over the next fifteen years the young priest, now called Don John Bosco, built an impressive community that cared for the poor youth of Turin.

He worked tirelessly, establishing residence halls, workshops for apprentices, and Latin schools to prepare men for the priesthood. By 1856, five hundred boys were attending his Sunday events and one hundred fifty were housed with him. There were four apprentice workshops and four Latin classes served by ten young priests. All gathered for worship and teaching in the Church of Saint Francis de Sales, which he had constructed for the children in 1852. Thus, Don Bosco was true to his dream. He used his extraordinary pastoral gifts to care for his boys as a shepherd cares for his flock.

The saint accomplished all of this against great odds. Landlords, city officials, and Turin's socialites often blocked his way because they were inconvenienced and somewhat frightened by his filthy, rambunctious horde of boys.

Even his fellow clergy gave him trouble. Once two of the saint's priest friends decided his fantastic visions were marks of insanity and developed a plot to get him confined to an asylum. The plan was to lure him into a carriage that would carry him off to a mental hospital. The priests arranged for attendants at the asylum to be sure to incarcerate, forcibly, if necessary, the occupant of the carriage. The priests then visited John Bosco, and after a brief conversation, invited him to take a ride in the country. Don Bosco, however, by divine intuition had read their scheme perfectly. As he and the others approached the carriage, he politely stepped aside and forced his two friends to get in, slamming the door behind them. "Quick!" he shouted to the driver. "To the asylum. Don't stop till you get there. You've got two dangerous characters locked inside." The driver rushed the priests to the institution, where several husky attendants restrained them. Despite the priests' protests, the aides locked them up for several uncomfortable hours before the mistake was discovered and they were released. Never again did they try to trick the saint.

To add to his difficulties, Don Bosco had very little money to work with. From his poverty, however, riches seemed to flow. When he had a need, he did everything humanly possible to meet it. Then he counted on God to intervene. And intervene God did, in instances too numerous to mention. Let me give just one representative example.

In 1866, as Don Bosco built the great church of Our Lady, Help of Christians, he regularly ran out of money. One day he needed four thousand francs to pay his contractors. By midmorning, benefactors had contributed one thousand francs. In the afternoon, Bosco wandered the streets, seeking a miracle for the rest. A wealthy man's servant approached him and asked the saint to visit his master, who had been bedridden for three years. Sensing his opportunity, Don Bosco went to the sick man's bedside.

"Reverend Father," the man said, "I need your prayers. I hurt so much that I can't move at all, and the doctors give me no hope. If I get even a little relief, I'll make a generous donation to your work."

"How fortunate!" said Don Bosco. "Today we need three thousand francs for construction of the church of Our Lady, Help of Christians."

"I couldn't possibly arrange that today." he said. " Besides, I'm too sick to go to the bank."

"And why shouldn't you get up and go to the bank?" the saint asked. "We need the money now. Nothing is impossible to God." Then he rounded up everyone in the house to pray for the man's healing.

With the whole household around him as witnesses, the man recovered instantaneously. He jumped out of bed and asked for his clothes. Dressed for the first time in months, he sat down to a huge lunch with many courses of rich food. Then, delighted to be out of the house, he went to the bank and returned shortly with the three thousand francs.

"I am completely cured," he exclaimed repeatedly.

"You take your money out of the bank," said Don Bosco, "and Our Lady, Help of Christians, takes you out of the bed."

The saint's dedicated service to others also occasioned miracles. In 1854, a cholera epidemic struck Turin. John Bosco assigned forty-four of his boys to tend the sick and carry victims to temporary hospitals. The boys worked tirelessly from October through December, bringing relief to many sick people. Miraculously, not a single one of them contracted the highly infectious disease.

A year later, Don Bosco decided to take three hundred juvenile offenders from their imprisonment in a reformatory for a day of recreation in a park. He got permission from Urban Ratazzi, the home minister of the country. Ratazzi was a leading opponent of the church, and Don Bosco hoped to intrigue him with a little miracle. The official feared that many boys might seize the opportunity to escape, but Don Bosco charmed him with many assurances, and finally he allowed the event. The boys had a great time in the open air, with games, sports, a picnic, and ferverinos from the priest, who had quickly become their hero. At the end of the day—to Ratazzi's great surprise—Don Bosco returned like a shepherd with his sheep. Mounted on a donkey and surrounded by a rowdy parade of boys, he had not lost a single one.

Don Bosco's supernatural knowledge was the most startling and discomfiting of his miraculous gifts. Contemporaries described his eyes as "penetrating." With a glance he could look into people's souls and read their spiritual state. Over the years, hundreds of boys were moved to repentance when he quietly urged them to confess a secret sin. Once an incredulous newcomer challenged the saint before the crowd of boys. "If Don Bosco knows any of my sins, he can tell them aloud," he said. Don Bosco leaned close to the boy's ear and whispered an accurate list of his sins. "You must have heard my confession at church this morning!" exclaimed the surprised youth. "I don't think so!" shouted all the boys. "Don Bosco has been with us the whole day."

In dreams and visions, Bosco foresaw the future. At least one hundred fifty of the saint's revelatory dreams are a matter of record. A vision of fiery tongues over a boy's head would tell him the young man was called to the priesthood. On many occasions a dream revealed to him the life span of a colleague or a boy's approaching death. He used the supernatural information to encourage his fellows to persevere through hard times. Whenever he foresaw an impending death, he did all he could to help the person die well. He composed an "exercise for a happy death," which he regularly had his boys recite as a means of focusing them on the serious side of life.

The saint had uncanny revelations of faraway events and situations. Once, in 1886, from Turin he supernaturally ferreted out a pedophile who was seducing boys many miles away at one of his schools in Barcelona. The priest in charge of the school testified later that Don Bosco had mysteriously appeared to him in a series of dreams and compelled him to confront and dismiss the man. Astounded and broken by Don Bosco's revelation, the offender confessed his wrongdoing and left the school.

Dreams also guided Don Bosco's work. He foresaw that he would assemble a large company of priests who would extend his ministry to the far ends of the earth. In 1854, he organized a band of his helpers, who took the name "Salesians," after Francis de Sales, Don Bosco's favorite saint. The church established the Salesians as a religious community in 1869. By 1875 Don Bosco was sending missionaries as far away as South America. In 1883, an incredible dream revealed to him the future worldwide extent of his communities. In it he envisioned automobiles, airplanes, and freeways as the means of transportation that would connect his widely scattered mission centers! This dream was realized early in the twentieth century, when thousands of Salesians were at work throughout the world.

I would have liked to have met John Bosco, to watch him firsthand with his boys. Perhaps his supreme generosity would be contagious and awaken a spirit of kindness in me. And I think about how I might have reacted to his spectacular miracles. His supernatural healings would have certainly impressed me, but prompted by my extreme caution, and to my detriment, I would probably have taken a wait-and-see attitude toward his prophecies.

And for sure, I would avoid looking Don John Bosco in the eye.

ᏅᏖᎳᏀ

Exercise for a Happy Death

When my feet, benumbed in death, shall warn me that my mortal course is drawing to a close—Merciful Jesus, have mercy on me!

When my eyes, dim and troubled at the approach of death, shall fix themselves on thee, my last and only support—Merciful Jesus, have mercy on me!

When my ears, soon to be shut forever to the words of men, shall be opened to hear your voice pronouncing the sentence of my irrevocable doom—Merciful Jesus, have mercy on me!

When I shall have lost the use of my senses; when the world shall have vanished from my sight; when my agonizing soul shall feel the sorrow of death—Merciful Jesus, have mercy on me!

—SAINT JOHN BOSCO

Part Five

∽᠁᠙

Miracles That Changed the Course of History

The saints give little thought to changing the world around them. They are too busy changing the world within them. They are not out to reform Caesar, but to conform themselves to Christ.

—CLARE BOOTH LUCE

Have you ever tried to find God's will for your life? Like me, you may have spent hours searching for wisdom about an important decision. On the whole, I think my time wrestling with this issue of God's will has been time well spent. But when I reflect on the lives of the saints, I wonder if there might be a better way to know the will of God.

Sometimes it seems I devote more energy looking for God's plan for my life than I do looking for God himself. I do believe he has a plan, but not the caricature that I sometimes make of it. Retreat master Martin Smith says that Christians are often mistaken in the way they try to learn God's will. "Do you really believe," he asks, "that God hides his will from us and expects us to search for it as though we are on a treasure hunt?"

Isn't knowing God's will more of a surrender than a search? We give ourselves to God. The desires of our hearts blend with his. His wanting becomes our wanting, says Martin Smith, and our plans give way to his. Look at the simple obedience of the saints and the divinely inspired fruit it bore.

When Francis Xavier said yes to God and no to his own plans, he unexpectedly accomplished something of great historical significance. He spread Christianity to the East, permanently affecting the lives of millions of people. Xavier's submission shows one way God keeps a hand in world events. One man's surrender allowed God to change the course of human history.

The same is true for Saint Clotilda and Saint Joan of Arc. Clotilda's submission to God brought her into a marriage with Clovis, the pagan king of the Franks. We still feel the effect of her patient and tender love for her husband. Her affection for Clovis helped persuade him to become a Christian, with his warriors and the whole nation soon following his example. Thus, Clotilda's obedience occasioned the introduction of Christianity into western Europe.

Joan of Arc's surrender to God put her in the forefront of world history. Where on earth, wondered the leaders of France, did this nineteen-year-old peasant girl get the idea she should lead an army? The idea, however, did not come from earth. From age twelve, Joan heard voices from heaven that said God wanted her to lead the French to victory. Saint Joan's obedience accomplished a task that seemed humanly impossible. The memory of her still touches the imagination and hearts of millions worldwide, perhaps more than any other saint.

The surrender of the saints gave God permission to intervene directly in human events. That accounts for the flow of signs and wonders in their wakes. You can see it in Saint Patrick. As a young man he traded his own wants for God's. What God wanted, it seemed, was the conversion of Ireland to Christianity. Saint Patrick did it in grand style. He upstaged magicians, baptized people, built churches, trained clergy, and educated young people. All the while he was guided by visions and dreams, and miracles swirled about him.

The saints make a pretty strong case for surrender as a strategy for knowing God's will. Maybe it's time to stop searching so hard, in order to let Christ shape our hearts in ways that enable us to both know and do what he wants.

಄

Miraculous Voices

Saint Joan of Arc (1412 — 1431)

ᏫᎥᎥ

Nearly all the saints had a "religious" task to perform,
and they had to leave the world, so as to be free to
accomplish it. But Joan breaks through this rule.

She was called to perform a purely worldly task, to free a people
from unendurable political misery, to set a rightful king on the throne,
to expel the enemy. She doesn't leave the world because of her
mission. Because of it she goes into the world, right into most
dangerous places, into the court, into the camp, into war.
—IDA COUDENHOVE

The church does not officially remember Joan of Arc as a martyr but as a virgin—the Maid of Orleans. Of course, Joan was a martyr, but not in the technical sense. Yes, she died because she did what she thought God wanted her to do. But she was killed, not for her faith but for her politics. Pagans did not execute her for refusing to worship their gods. Infidels did not slay her for defying them. Political enemies burned her at the stake for defeating them at war.

Paradoxically, Christian people, good and bad alike, cheered at her demise. Other Christians wept. This incongruity may trouble us, but Joan would have expected it. The war she fought embroiled French Christians against English Christians. We, too, have waged wars like that, pitting Christian against Christian. And just as we may have felt that God was on our side, Joan believed God was with the French. The judges who condemned her asked if the heavenly voices she followed to war spoke in English. She replied tartly: "Why should they speak in English when they were not on the English side?"

Joan of Arc was born into the violent times of the fifteenth century. During her childhood, King Henry V of England had invaded France and seized Normandy. He laid claim to the crown of the French king, Charles VI, who was mentally ill. Paralyzed by civil war between the duke of Burgundy and the duke of Orleans, the French could not put up much of a defense. The latter, Charles, duke of Orleans, was heir to the French throne. Things worsened when Charles's agents murdered the duke of Burgundy. The Burgundians reacted by becoming England's allies.

Eventually, Burgundian mercenaries brought the war home to Joan's family. The raiders sacked the little village of Domrémy, forcing them to flee. Thus, the indiscriminate brutality of war disrupted Joan of Arc's pleasant childhood to acquaint her with fear.

Both the English and French kings died in 1422, but their successors pursued the war. The English, with Burgundian support, marched steadily across France, taking one town at a time. Charles, duke of Orleans, was not yet crowned or anointed king. The enemy controlled the road to Rheims, the traditional site where French kings were crowned. Regarding the situation as hopeless, the future king languished with his court near Orleans.

In 1424, when Joan was only twelve years old, the great miracle of her life unfolded. One summer day in her father's garden, she heard an audible voice accompanied by a bright light. "At first I was very much frightened," she said later. "The voice came toward the hour of noon. I had fasted the preceding day. I heard the voice on my right hand, in the direction of the church. I seldom hear it without seeing a light. The light always appears on the side from which I hear the voice."

She identified the speaker as Michael the Archangel. Subsequently, he spoke to her many times, gradually revealing a preposterous mission. "You have been chosen to restore the kingdom of France," said the voice, "and to protect King Charles." She was to accomplish these things at the head of the army! Imagine the terror and confusion the archangel's messages must have caused young Joan.

Michael also told her that Saint Catherine and Saint Margaret would appear to her. God was sending these saints, he said, so she must obey their directions. Over the next seven years, Michael, Catherine, and Margaret are said to have visited Joan frequently, sometimes several times a day. Not only could she see and hear her heavenly messengers, she could also touch and smell them. At her trial she testified that she physically embraced the saints and that they had a pleasant fragrance.

Joan found the visions comforting, but they also put her under great stress. Fear of her strict father compelled her to keep them secret, except to confide in her parish priest. The messages must have both thrilled and troubled her. The revelations conflicted with reality. How would a simple peasant girl accomplish such imposing, if not impossible, tasks?

By May 1428, Joan's voices had become relentless and specific. They directed her to go at once to Robert Baudricourt, the commander of the royal forces in a town nearby. Reluctantly, she obeyed. Baudricourt, however, greeted her with laughter, telling her what she needed was a good spanking from her father.

At that time, conditions were deteriorating for the French. The English had put Orleans under siege, and the stronghold was in grave danger. Joan's voices became more insistent. "But I am merely a girl! I cannot ride a horse or wield a weapon!" she protested.

"It is God who commands it!" came the reply.

Resisting no more, Joan secretly made her way back to Baudricourt. When she arrived she told the commander a fact she could only have known by revelation. She said the French army—on that very day—had suffered a defeat near Orleans. Joan urged him to send her to Orleans so that she might fulfill her mission. When official reports confirmed Joan's word, Baudricourt finally took her seriously and sent her to Charles.

Charles kept Joan waiting three days before he admitted her to court. When Joan entered, the king was in disguise, hiding among his courtiers. But Joan went directly to him. The voices had given her a secret sign, which when she communicated it to Charles, convinced him of her authenticity. Pressed by suspicious advisers, he had Joan examined by a team of theologians at Poitiers. They discerned no problems and recommended that Charles make judicious use of her services.

Thus the way was cleared for Joan of Arc to fulfill her divinely appointed task. Joan was outfitted with white armor and provided a special standard bearing the names "Jesus" and "Mary." The banner depicted two kneeling angels offering a *fleur de lis* to God. On April 29, 1429, Joan led her army into Orleans. Miraculously, the saint rallied the town. By May 8, the French had captured the English forts and lifted the siege. An arrow had penetrated the armor over Joan's breast, but the injury was not serious enough to keep her out of the battle. Everything, including the wound, occurred exactly as Joan had prophesied before the campaign.

A peasant maiden had defeated the army of a mighty kingdom, a humiliation that craved revenge.

The way to Rheims was now open. Joan urged the immediate coronation of the king, but the reluctant French leaders dragged their feet. Finally, however, at Rheims on July 17, 1429, Charles VII was anointed King of France. The Maid of Orleans stood triumphantly at his side. Joan had accomplished her mission.

During the battles at Orleans, the voices had told Joan she had only a little time left. And so her shameful end lurked ominously in the shadows. Later, she sustained a serious arrow wound in the thigh during an unsuccessful attack on Paris. After spending the winter in court, in May 1430, she led a force to relieve Compiègne, which the Burgundians had under siege. Her effort failed and she was captured.

Through the summer and fall, Joan was the prisoner of the duke of Burgundy. The French, apparently ungrateful, made no effort to rescue her or obtain her release. On November 21, 1430, the Burgundians sold Joan to the English for a large sum. They were quite eager to punish the maiden who had bested them.

The English could not execute Joan for winning, but they could impose capital punishment for sorcery or heresy. For several months she was chained in a cell in the castle at Rouen, where five coarse guards taunted her constantly. In February 1431, Joan appeared before a tribunal headed by Peter Cauchon, bishop of Beauvais, who was an avaricious and wicked man.

Joan had no chance for a fair trial. She stood alone before devious judges, an uneducated girl conducting her own defense. The panel interrogated her six times in public, nine times in private. They questioned her closely about her visions, voices, male dress, faith, and submissiveness to the church. Giving good, sometimes even unexpectedly clever answers, Joan handled herself courageously. However, the judges took advantage of her lack of education and tripped her up on a few slippery theological points. The panel packed its summary with her damaging replies and condemned her with that unfair report. They declared that her revelations were demonic.

The tribunal decided that unless Joan recanted she was to die as a heretic. At first she plainly refused. But later, when she was taken before a huge throng, she seems to have made some sort of retraction. When she was returned to prison, however, somehow she was tricked into wearing men's clothing, which she had promised to forsake.

Cauchon visited her, observed her dress, and determined that she had fallen back into error. Joan, her strength renewed, then repudiated her earlier retraction. She declared that God had truly commissioned her and that her voices had come from him. "Be of good cheer!" Cauchon said to an English lord as he left the castle. "We'll get her yet!" Cauchon reported these events to the tribunal. On his word, on May 29, 1431, having condemned Joan of Arc as a relapsed heretic, the judges remanded her to the state for execution. The next morning she was taken into Rouen's public square and burned at the stake.

Like Jesus, Joan of Arc seemed to end her life in failure.

Twenty-three years later, however, Joan's mother and brothers asked that her case be reopened. Pope Callistus III appointed a commission to review the matter. In 1456, the new panel repudiated the trial and verdict and completely restored Joan's reputation. Once again her piety and exemplary conduct had triumphed.

Few Christians hear audible, heaven-sent voices. I know I don't. Joan was one of those rare exceptions who did. She obeyed what she perceived to be God's directions, and against all odds, achieved the purpose she was given. Though I've never heard an audible voice, now and then I sense something God wants of me. Doesn't that also happen to you? Perhaps Joan's example will reach down through the centuries to touch and encourage us to listen closely for whatever God wants to say to us today.

ᏮᎷᎥᎿᏬ

The Death of Saint Joan

And when they had come into the marketsquare there was a great concourse of many thousands awaiting them, and in the midst was a heap of mortar very high, hardened to stone, and a tall stake standing in it, and the faggots piled around it. These, after one deputed had preached at her, she mounted without faltering, and was chained to the stake. But being there, above the people, and seen by all, she forgave her enemies and begged each priest in that multitude to say one mass for her soul.

Then she asked for a cross, and an English soldier bound two sticks together and held it up for her to take, which she kissed and put into the bosom of her white robe. She asked also for a crucifix from the church at hand, and this was found and given her. And when she had held this up before her and kissed it also fervently, while the English lords clamored at the delay, the torch was set to the faggots, and in the midst of the smoke they heard her proclaiming firmly that indeed her mission was of God, and they heard her praying to the saints; till, in a very little while, a loud voice came from the midst of the burning, the holy name Jesus, called so loudly that every man heard it to the very ends of the square. And after that there was silence, and no sound but the crackling of the fire.

—HILAIRE BELLOC

MIRACLES OVER MAGIC

Saint Patrick (389–461)

〰️

*Ireland, which never had the knowledge of God, but up till
now always adored idols and things unclean—how are they now
made a people of the Lord, and are called children of God?
The sons of the Scots and the daughters of their chieftains
are seen to become monks and virgins of Christ.*

—SAINT PATRICK

Our family wears green on Saint Patrick's Day. Or else we answer to the lady of the house. Her March 17 excesses have included making perfectly good food unpalatable with green dye. Sometimes I think my dear Irish wife's blood must run emerald.

I wonder what the saint himself would make of the shenanigans that mark his feast day in the United States. Would Patrick be comfortable with the festivities of his annual commemoration? Would he wear a shamrock? Wield a shillelagh? Dance a jig? Recite limericks? Eat green food and drink green beer?

I will not say that Patrick would not enjoy all that hoopla. After all, historians call him the first true Irishman. So we can expect that, like his compatriots, he knew how to celebrate. Perhaps, however, Patrick would like to see us enhance his remembrance day with some specifically Christian customs, as many do in Ireland. Like taking time out to pray or to study the Bible or to share a word of faith with a neighbor. For prayer, Scripture, and evangelism were the real hallmarks of his life.

Patrick first came to Ireland as a slave in 403, when raiders tore him and many others from their homes in Roman Britain. For six years, near a mountain in northern Ireland, Patrick herded swine for his pagan master. In his *Confession*, the saint says that his bondage was a time of spiritual strengthening. "My love and fear of God," he said, "increased greatly, and my faith grew, and my spirit was stirred up." He spent his days and his nights praying. "Before dawn, in snow and frost and rain, I used to be aroused to prayer," he recalled. "Nor was there any tepidity in me, such as I now feel, because then the spirit was fervent within me." That admission of spiritual apathy attracts me to Patrick and comforts me. For all of us who feel that our youthful passion has strangely cooled, he is a hopeful sign.

One night, Patrick heard a heavenly voice in his dreams that revealed he would soon return to his homeland. Later on, the voice spoke of a ship two hundred miles away that was ready to carry him to Britain. Patrick fled from his master and walked the long distance to the boat. When he arrived, the captain refused at first to take him. After Patrick prayed, however, the captain reconsidered and gave him passage.

The ship reached shore in three days. Then Patrick and the sailors trekked for a month through rough terrain. When their food ran out, the shipmaster challenged him to pray to his God for help. "Turn earnestly," said Patrick, "and with all your hearts to the Lord my God, to whom nothing is impossible." Just then a herd of swine appeared on the road, and the pigs soon became a hearty barbecue. Until Patrick left the seamen a month later, they did not lack for food or anything else.

Patrick was about twenty-two years old when he was reunited with his family. They welcomed him warmly, hoping he would never again be separated from them. But that was not to be. He soon received dreams that urged him to return to Ireland. "I heard," wrote the saint, "the voices of those who dwelt beside the wood of Focluth, which is by the western sea. And thus they cried, as if with one mouth: 'We beseech you, holy youth, to come and walk once more among us.'" Patrick understood that God was calling him to take the Gospel to Ireland. In fact, to become the Apostle of Ireland.

Patrick went to France, where he worked twenty-one years preparing for his mission. Establishing the Christian church in Ireland would require many things. He had to be ready to proclaim the Good News to a pagan people. He would have to be able to provide for the Christian formation and care of his converts. Wherever he founded communities, he would need to recruit and train a native clergy and build and equip churches. Above all, he must have the strength and savvy to overturn the resistance of the druids, the priests who dominated the Irish with their magic.

Thus, Patrick devoted himself to acquiring spiritual disciplines and practical skills for three years at the monastery of Lerins. Then he spent fifteen more at Auxerre, where the great monk and bishop, Saint Germanus, was his mentor. Patrick did not become a scholar but a church-planter. Later, he keenly felt his lack of education and often bemoaned it. However, he knew that for his task he needed pastoral wisdom more than scholarship. During this time, Patrick was ordained deacon and priest. Ireland's first bishop, Saint Palladius, died in 431, after only one year of service. Patrick was consecrated as bishop to succeed him, and he launched his divinely appointed enterprise in 432.

The pivotal event in Saint Patrick's ministry occurred in 433 on the first Easter after his return. He was determined to win the support of the High-King Laoghaire, the powerful ruler of central Ireland, whose blessing would open doors for him everywhere. His resolve to gain the king's support precipitated a dramatic confrontation with leading druids. The saint's triumph over them in a contest of spiritual power versus magic secured the success of his mission at its outset.

It happened on the night before Easter. Laoghaire was celebrating a pagan festival at Tara, his base in central Ireland. By law, no one was permitted to kindle a fire until the ceremonial beacon on the Royal Hill was lighted. Miles away atop the Hill of Slane, Patrick had gathered his followers for the Easter vigil. Unaware of the prohibition against fires, Patrick opened the liturgy by striking the new fire, the vivid symbol of Christ's resurrection. Had he known of the prohibition, he would probably have ignored it anyway.

King Laoghaire, his barons, and druids saw Patrick's paschal fire and were enraged. The druids, sensing imminent danger, warned the king that he must extinguish the fire immediately. If not, said one prophetically, "it will never be extinguished in Ireland. Moreover, it will outshine all the fires we light. And he who has kindled it will conquer us all." So the king and eight chariots full of warriors headed for Patrick's camp.

Upon arrival the king summoned Patrick and demanded an explanation. The saint responded with a simple summary of the Gospel. When Drochu, a leading druid, made fun of the Christian mysteries, Patrick prayed aloud that he be punished. With that, Drochu was swooped high into the air and dropped to his death. The warriors then attempted to capture Patrick, but he prayed they would be scattered. A dark cloud and a whirlwind descended on them, causing a panic in which many perished.

The king cowered at this demonstration of might. In his fright, he made a hollow pretense of acknowledging God and invited Patrick to speak about the Christian faith to his barons at Tara. Then he left Slane, planning to lie in wait to ambush Patrick and his associates. When Patrick and his band passed by, however, they were invisible to Laoghaire and his would-be assassins. It is said that as the Christians escaped they chanted for the first time the saint's famous "Breastplate." The prayer calls upon the power of the Trinity, the Incarnation, the angels, and all of heaven against every conceivable danger. In the following years, Patrick would pray it often.

On Easter day, King Laoghaire held a banquet at Tara as part of the pagan religious festival. Patrick and five companions mystified the gathering by passing through locked doors and appearing in their midst. Invited to sit near the king, Patrick was then given a drink that Lucat-Mael, the chief druid, had laced with poison. Discerning the mischief, Patrick made a cross over the cup and the beverage froze, with the drop of poison alone remaining liquid. Everyone watched as Patrick poured it on the table. He blessed the cup again, and his drink returned to normal.

Thus humiliated before his peers, Lucat-Mael sought to redeem himself. He challenged Patrick to a public contest of wonders on the plain of Tara, where many Irish could watch. First, the druid is said to have magically filled the plain waist-high with snow.

"We see the snow," said Patrick. "Now, remove it."

"I cannot until tomorrow," said the druid.

"Then, you are powerful for evil, but not for good. Not so with me," said Patrick. He stretched out his hands, once again carving a cross in the air. Instantly, the snow disappeared without a trace. The crowd cheered.

For his next magical stunt, the druid shrouded the plain in total darkness. Once again he was unable to reverse his trick until the next day. Patrick prayed and with a blessing dismissed the darkness. This time, the onlookers erupted with praise for Patrick's God.

To settle the issue once and for all, Patrick proposed the third contest, a trial by fire. The Druid, covered by Patrick's cloak, would be locked in a greenwood hut. Benignus, Patrick's young disciple, wearing Lucat-Mael's cloak, would be placed in a hut made of dry wood. Then both huts would be burned to the ground. All accepted the terms, and with the two men in place, the huts were torched. This test had a marvelous outcome. Flames consumed the greenwood hut and the druid, but Patrick's cloak was not even singed. Benignus and his hut remained untouched by the fire, but Lucat-Mael's cloak was burned to ashes.

Patrick's miraculous encounters with the druids were so spectacular that some modern historians discount them as legends. But extraordinary as the miracles were, the earliest documents reported them as facts. Saint Patrick's wonders set the stage for the conversion of Ireland. Why should he not have expected divine interventions at such significant moments in his missionary venture?

Even though Patrick had exposed the emptiness of Laoghaire's religion, the ruler did not become a Christian. He made two decisions, however, that significantly advanced Patrick's work. He gave Patrick permission to preach the Gospel in Ireland, and he ensured Patrick's personal safety.

From that time, the saint criss-crossed the island, making disciples everywhere he went. In a relatively short time, he baptized tens of thousands of converts and built hundreds of churches, staffing them with Irish priests and deacons. He founded many monasteries and schools to care for the passionate youths who decided to follow him to Christ. In 444, scarcely a dozen years after Patrick arrived, he established Ireland's first cathedral church at Armagh, which quickly became a center of Christian education and church administration.

By the time of Patrick's death in 461, he had completely dislodged the ancient paganism. The whole island had become thoroughly and permanently Christian. Now, that's a miracle I challenge anyone to dismiss.

ᎧᎿᏇᎧ

Christ Is All in All

Christ with me, Christ before me,
Christ behind me, Christ within me,
Christ beneath me, Christ above me,
Christ at my right, Christ at my left.

Christ in the head of everyone who thinks of me,
Christ in the mouth of everyone who speaks to me,
Christ in every eye that sees me,
Christ in every ear that hears me.

—FROM SAINT PATRICK'S *BREASTPLATE*

![decorative border of triangular shapes]

MIRACLES IN THE "DARK" AGES

Saint Clotilda, Saint Vedast, and Saint Remi (fifth century)

᷍

The conversion of Clovis issued in results of
profound importance to mankind.
—DEAN MILMAN

Occasionally God may work a miracle privately to benefit a single soul. But usually, when he intervenes in one life, he causes ripples in the lives of others. The instantaneous cure of a child's brain tumor, for example, may generate a spiritual renewal in an entire family. And once in a while a miracle's ripple effect swells into a mighty wave that affects millions. This was the case with the miracles that influenced Clovis, king of the Franks, to become a Christian. The story of these events may convince you that the Dark Ages were not as dark as we sometimes imagine.

Key players in this story are

Clovis, the pagan warrior, who became king of the Franks at age fifteen in A.D. 481.

Saint Clotilda, the princess from Burgundy, who became Clovis's wife and queen.

Saint Vedast, a priest and gifted teacher in the town of Toul, who educated Clovis in the faith.

Saint Remi, bishop of Rheims, who would become known as the Apostle of the Franks.

The late fifth century was a tumultuous era in Europe. Rampant decadence was imploding the aging Roman Empire everywhere. Visigoths, Ostrogoths, and other marauding barbarians thundered through the countryside. They hastened the empire's collapse, leaving death and devastation in their paths. Many of these tribes had been converted to Arianism, the remarkably resilient heresy that held that Jesus Christ was not God, but merely an exceptional human being. All of the European continent was thus in grave material and spiritual danger.

Shortly after Clovis became king, he began to lead the Franks in wars of conquest against his neighbors on every side. Soon he had built a sturdy little kingdom in northern France. In 491 he married Clotilda, a wise and resourceful woman, who was an orthodox Christian. At once she began to work quietly for the spiritual conquest of Clovis himself. The saintly queen prayed for her king and conducted herself as a loving, supportive wife. Clotilda told Clovis all about Christ, the God-King she worshiped. In her efforts to win Clovis to Christ, she sought the counsel and help of Saint Remi. Clotilda's persistence bore fruit of world historical consequence.

In 496, Clovis defended his kingdom against an invasion by the Alemanni, a fierce Germanic tribe, which had crossed the Rhine near

Cologne. When it appeared that his troops would soon be overwhelmed, Clovis appealed to Clotilda's God. "O Christ, whom Clotilda invokes as son of the living God," he cried, "I beg your help. I have called upon my gods and they are powerless. If you deliver me from my enemies, I promise I'll be baptized in your name." God seemed to answer Clovis convincingly, because the tide of battle suddenly turned in his favor. The enemy turned tail, leaving Clovis and his men victorious.

To fulfill his vow to Christ, Clovis and his entourage headed toward Rheims, where he intended to be baptized by Saint Remi. At Toul he met Saint Vedast, who joined the company in order to instruct the king in preparation for his baptism. On the way God startled Clovis and his men with a miracle.

When they reached a bridge at the Aisne River, they encountered a blind man who begged Vedast to give him sight. Vedast laid his right hand on the man's eyes and prayed, "Lord Jesus, you who are the true light, who opened the eyes of the man born blind, open also the eyes of this man, that the people may understand that you are the only God who works miracles in heaven and earth." The blind man's eyes opened instantly. This healing strengthened Clovis's resolve to become a Christian and swayed some of his warriors toward Christ.

Perhaps God cured this man's physical blindness as a sign that he was about to begin a greater cure of a spiritual blindness—the long-term evangelization of the Franks. Perhaps, too, he was signaling that Saint Vedast would play an important role in bringing the light of Christ to Europe's darkness.

Meanwhile, at Rheims Clotilda and Remi had prepared for the king's baptism, and everything was ready when the entourage arrived. Clovis, however, had become reluctant to approach baptism. He was concerned that his people might not be willing to forsake their gods. He decided to assemble his chiefs and warriors and address them about his desire to acknowledge Christ. But before he could speak, the tribal leaders shouted, "We renounce our dead gods and are ready to follow the living God whom Remi preaches." So Remi and Vedast instructed them and prepared them for baptism.

Clotilda had arranged for a dazzling celebration. The street approaching the church was lined with colorful banners, and the church and baptistry were decorated with gilt tapestries and illumined with thousands of twinkling candles. A great procession, with candidates carrying crosses, led the king to the baptismal font. Remi greeted Clovis with these striking words: "Humble yourself, my king. Worship what you have burned, and burn what you have worshiped."

During the ceremony, Remi discovered that the oil of chrism for the anointing was missing. The servant bearing it had been unable to penetrate the crowds around the baptistry. Remi prayed, and miraculously a dove appeared bearing a small bottle of chrism. It is said that this vial of oil, known in French as *la Sainte Ampoule*, was used throughout history to consecrate the kings of France until it was destroyed during the French Revolution. Maybe this heaven-sent oil announced God's intention to strengthen spiritually the kings who would preside over the spread of the Gospel in Europe.

Shortly after the baptism of Clovis, Remi baptized three thousand of the king's soldiers and their families. This was only the beginning of the saint's massive task of establishing the Franks in the Christian faith. With the support of Clovis and Clotilda, he presided over the evangelization of the kingdom. For the work, Remi enlisted many bishops and priests. Among these was Vedast, who as the bishop of Arras, labored nearly forty years, patiently indoctrinating the people of that region in the Christian religion.

What was the greatest miracle that occurred among the Franks? Was it the healing of the blind man at the Aisne? The dove bearing the chrism? The conversion of Clovis? What do you think? Maybe the real miracle was the planting of the seed of faith among the Franks. The gradual evangelization of the Franks into orthodox Christianity slowly eliminated paganism and prevented Europe from falling prey to Arianism. Thus, three little-known saints, supported by God's miraculous intervention, lit a bright light in the Dark Ages.

ᏨᎥᎥᎥᏤ

Saints on Purpose

In his saints God is manifest as power, more powerful than created energies, complete and final Reality, more real than the partial reality of creatures. By finding God and by his union with God the saint has found the only satisfying explanation of the world and human life, the only satisfying purpose for which to live, act, and suffer. He has found a happiness independent of life's vicissitudes, a security no external disasters can shake, integrity and order, confidence without arrogance, peace in activity, a fixed end combined with flexibility of means, detachment from creatures combined with appreciation of them. For he has found God, who is wholly other than the world, but is its source and positive being.

—E. I. Watkin

A MIRACLE WITHIN

Saint Francis Xavier (1506–1552)

᧖

*If anyone would come after me, he must deny himself and take up his
cross and follow me. For whoever wants to save his life will lose it, but
whoever loses his life for me and for the gospel will save it.*
—MARK 8:34–35

Francis Xavier had planned to devote himself to the intellectual life,
but at a strategic moment he surrendered to God, who had long and
patiently pursued him. That surrender changed the course of his life—
and the course of history as well. Even Ignatius Loyola, the leader of the
new Jesuit community, had planned to deploy Francis as a scholar. But
India beckoned, and Ignatius reluctantly sent Francis to preach the
Gospel there. Thus, the man who had planned on a leisurely intellectual life became a missionary apostle, perhaps second only to Saint Paul.

In 1525, Francis left Xavier, his mother's castle near Pamplona in
Navarre, to study at the University of Paris. He enrolled at the College
of Saint Barbara, where he pursued an unwaveringly successful academic

career. Within three short years he had earned his degree and was lecturing in philosophy.

At Saint Barbara, circumstances put Xavier's spiritual career on course. Through his roommate, Saint Peter Faber, Francis became a friend of Saint Ignatius Loyola. This relationship gradually revolutionized his life.

Ignatius was seeking gifted men to join him in pursuit of a radical vision. Loyola's dream was to form a spiritual army committed to advancing the work of Christ. Faber was one of his first recruits, but Francis held out for six years. Attracted to Loyola's ideals, he was yet reluctant to make them his own. In fact, he was wary of Ignatius's desire to build a community of disciples because it threatened the autonomy he would have as a church-supported scholar.

One day in 1533, however, things came to a crisis. Francis had just been appointed a canon at the cathedral of Pamplona with a secure income from church property. As he reflected on his dream-come-true, he overheard Loyola and Faber discussing their plans in the next room. At that moment Francis mysteriously felt all his resistance to Ignatius slip away. A desire to throw in with Loyola captivated Xavier's heart and dismissed his own life plan.

As the saint reached his decision, unbidden, the text of Genesis 12:1 crossed his mind: "Leave your country, your people and your father's household and go to the land I will show you." That verse gave Francis a prophetic inkling of the unanticipated direction his life would take.

In 1534, Francis Xavier was among the first seven men to decide to formally join Ignatius Loyola's community. They were the first Jesuits, and Francis was ordained a priest three years later. Loyola had long-term plans to deploy Xavier as a scholar and teacher, but circumstances derailed them. From the beginning, the Jesuits were in high demand, and

Ignatius had to scramble to meet all the requests. King John III of Portugal asked for six men to do missionary work in the Portuguese territories in India. Ignatius said he could spare two: Simon Rodriguez and Nicholas Bobadilla, who were to sail to Goa in 1541. At the last moment, however, Bobadilla became seriously ill. With some hesitance and uneasiness, Ignatius asked Francis to go in his place. Thus, Xavier accidentally found his life as an apostle to the East.

Xavier believed no one was more ill-equipped than he to take the Gospel overseas. But he was wrong. En route from Lisbon to Goa, Francis already displayed the cheerfulness and generosity that became the trademarks of his work. His personal charm made friends of the unlikeliest and toughest seamen on the ship. Then he engaged them in "apostolic conversations," seeking to win them for Christ.

Aboard ship he served others so tirelessly that, exhausted, he became dangerously ill himself. But he would not heed doctors' warnings to take care of himself. Once, he put a delirious and dying sailor in his own bed and lay down himself on a plank. Later, he was found conversing with the man, who had miraculously recovered his senses as soon as he was put into Francis' bed. The sailor died that evening, after confessing his sins and receiving Holy Communion. "His good end," said one observer, "caused the Father great happiness. Indeed, he always looked happy, no matter what his sufferings and burdens."

Xavier arrived in India in 1542. For the next decade he labored selflessly to plant the seeds of Christianity over thousands of miles from Goa as far as Kyoto, Japan. He died in 1552 while trying to smuggle himself into China, which was closed to missionaries.

The saint's missionary methods were primitive. When he arrived in a village, he rang a bell in the streets to summon the children and the idle. He taught them the Creed, the Ten Commandments, the Our

Father, and other common prayers. Using little songs that the children loved to sing, he instructed them in Christian doctrine. Then, when people expressed simple faith in the creed, he baptized them.

Some believe that Francis Xavier had a miraculous gift of languages that enabled him to communicate fluently with everyone, but that was not the case. Francis struggled with foreign languages and was barely able to express the creed, commandments, and prayers in Tamil and other native languages. He had to rely on makeshift interpreters and translators, so he was never completely sure he had accurately communicated his message. The real miracle of tongues was that Xavier spread the Gospel so far and to so many tens of thousands with so little grasp of their languages.

Miracles of healing, however, occurred frequently in his ministry to poor villages. Once, while traveling through a pagan territory, Francis learned of a woman who had been three days in labor and was probably near death. The midwives and sorcerers were treating her with superstitious incantations. Xavier went to the woman's home and called on the name of Christ to heal her. "I began with the Creed," he wrote to Ignatius, "which my companion translated into Tamil. By the mercy of God, the woman came to believe in the articles of faith. I asked whether she desired to become a Christian, and she replied that she would most willingly become one. Then I read excerpts from the gospels in that house, where, I think, they were never heard before. I then baptized the woman." Miraculously, as soon as Francis had baptized the woman, she was healed and gave birth to a healthy baby.

The woman's family was so touched by this divine intervention that they invited Francis to instruct and baptize all of them, including the newborn. News then traveled quickly throughout the village. A representative of the raja, the overlord, gave the village elders clearance to allow Francis to proclaim Christ there. "First, I baptized the chief men of the place and their families," he wrote, "and afterwards the rest of the people, young and old."

In another village, Francis was besieged by crowds who wanted him to pray for ailing family members. The saint was overwhelmed with missionary and teaching duties, so he enlisted some enthusiastic children to minister to the sick. He sent the children to the homes of the ill and had them gather the family and neighbors. He trained them to proclaim the Creed and assure the sick that if they believed, they would be cured. Thus, Xavier not only responded to requests for prayer but managed to spread Christian doctrine throughout the village. Because the sick and their families had faith, he said, "God has shown great mercy to them, healing them in both body and soul." The children of the village had become little miracle workers.

Some think the following story is only a winsome legend, but I think God allowed this playful miracle to highlight the spirit of the saint's life. Once, when Xavier and his companions were sailing to Baramua in Malaysia, a violent storm threatened to sink their boat. Francis removed a finger-length crucifix from his neck and dipped it in the water. Immediately the sea calmed. But to his great disappointment, Francis let the small cross slip from his fingers, and it was carried off by the waves.

The day after the storm, Francis and his friends disembarked and were walking along the shore toward Baramua. After they had gone about a half mile, a crab scurried out of the water, bearing a small object in its claws. It approached Francis and returned the tiny crucifix to him!

Francis Xavier's life was like that little wonder. The life he had envisioned slipped away. The life he found cost him everything. In his passion for spreading the Gospel, in his simple obedience, in his thoughtless disregard for himself, the saint was a near-perfect imitation of Christ.

ᕙᗯᕗ

Prayer of Surrender

O my God! Teach me to be generous; to give and not to count the cost; to fight and not to heed the wounds; to toil and not to seek for rest; to labor and not to seek for any reward save that of doing your blessed will.

—Saint Ignatius Loyola

Afterword

⚭

Lives Touched by the Supernatural

I have noticed an intriguing thread running through the lives of several saints we have observed. They were touched by God in extraordinary ways when they prayed the ancient hymn, the *Veni Creator Spiritus*, to the Holy Spirit.

The hymn is attributed to Rabanus Maurus, who lived in ninth-century Germany. He was a saintly scholar, abbot, and archbishop. The prayer came to be used in the liturgy for Pentecost, and religious communities all over Europe took it up.

The *Veni Creator Spiritus* marked the moment when Clare of Assisi made her radical commitment to Christ. Saint Francis and his brothers met the lovely runaway at the door of Saint Mary of the Angels. As they escorted her to the altar, where she embraced the Gospel, they chanted the beautiful hymn to the Holy Spirit.

If we can believe Saint Teresa of Avila's harsh self-evaluation, her early years as a nun bogged down in mediocrity. She says her spiritual life only began to flourish when a spiritual director required her to pray daily the *Veni Creator Spiritus*. Shortly after Teresa began to pray it, the saint experienced her first ecstasy. The hymn seemed to open her spiritual ears to a divine voice within, which seemed to say, "I will not have you hold conversations with men but with angels."

The *Veni Creator Spiritus* also occasioned a deepening of Saint Lutgarde's mysticism. Biographer Thomas of Cantimpré reported that one Pentecost, when the hymn was chanted, observers saw Lutgarde mysteriously transported in prayer. They said she appeared to float off the floor. Thomas commented that the saint's body momentarily seemed to share in the supernatural privileges of her spirit that was elevated heavenward.

Scripture describes the Holy Spirit as our Advocate, Counselor, Helper, Intercessor, and Teacher. He is the One the Father sends to intervene in human lives. He is often depicted as a dove descending gently to us. A line in the *Veni Creator Spiritus* calls him "the finger of God's right hand." Thus, for centuries, the church has seen the Spirit as the touch of the supernatural in our lives.

Here is the full text of the *Veni Creator Spiritus**:

> Come, Creator, Spirit, come
> from your bright heavenly throne,
> come take possession of our souls,
> and make them all your own.
>
> You who are called the Paraclete,
> best gift of God above,
> the living spring, the vital fire
> sweet christ'ning and true love.
>
> You who are sev'nfold in your grace,
> finger of God's right hand;
> his promise, teaching little ones
> to speak and understand.

---

*Adapted from *Hymns for the Year* (1896), translator anonymous.

O guide our minds with your blest light,
with love our hearts inflame;
and with your strength, which ne'er decays,
confirm our mortal frame.

Far from us drive our deadly foe;
true peace unto us bring;
and through all perils lead us safe
beneath your sacred wing.

Through you may we the Father know,
through you th' eternal Son,
and you the Spirit of them both,
thrice-blessed Three in One.

All glory to the Father be,
with his co-equal Son;
the same to you, great Paraclete,
while endless ages run.

Perhaps this hymn is the best thing you can take away from this book. If we really want to be like the saints, we won't look for miracles. Neither will we chase after spiritual experiences. Rather, we will let God's Holy Spirit touch our lives.

Index

⟨∞⟩

Saints and Their Feast Days

Saint Saturus (d. 203)	March 6
Venerable Solanus Casey (1870–1957)	July 31
Saint Teresa of Avila (1515–1582)	October 15
Saint Theresa Margaret (1747–1770)	March 11
Saint Vedast (d. 539)	February 6
Saint Vincent Ferrer (1350–1419)	April 5

Bibliography

Auffray, A., S.D.B. *Saint John Bosco*. Blaisdon, U.K.: Salesian Publications, 1930.

Belloc, Hilaire. *Saint Joan*. Boston: Little, Brown and Company, 1929.

Broderick, James, S. J. *Saint Francis Xavier*. New York: The Wicklow Press, 1952.

Bury, J. B. *The Life of Saint Patrick and His Place in History*. London: Macmillan and Co., 1905.

Cantor, Marvin. *The Origins of Christianity in Bohemia*. Evanston, IL: Northwestern University Press, 1990.

Cavallini, Giuliana. *Saint Martin de Porres: Apostle of Charity*. Rockford, IL: Tan Books & Publishers, Inc., 1979.

S[ister] M[ary]C[atherine]. *Angel of the Judgment: a Life of Vincent Ferrer*. Notre Dame, IN: Ave Maria Press, 1954.

DeRobeck, Nesta. *Saint Clare of Assisi*. Milwaukee, WI: The Bruce Publishing Company, 1951.

Derum, James Patrick. *The Porter of Saint Bonaventure's: The Life of Father Solanus Casey, Capuchin*. Detroit: The Fidelity Press, 1968.

Dorcy, Sr. Mary Jean, O.P. *Saint Dominic*. Rockford, IL: Tan Books and Publishers, 1982.

DuBoulay, Shirley. *Teresa of Avila: Her Story*. Ann Arbor, MI: Servant Publications, 1995.

Freemantle, Anne. *Saints Alive! The Lives of Thirteen Heroic Saints*. Garden City, NY: Doubleday & Company, 1978.

Ghéon, Henri. *Saint Vincent Ferrer*. New York: Sheed & Ward, 1939.

Healy, John. *The Life and Writings of Saint Patrick*. Dublin: M. H. Gill & Son, 1905.

Kearns, J. C., O.P. *The Life of Blessed Martin de Porres*. New York: P. J. Kennedy & Sons, 1937.

Luce, Clare Boothe, ed. *Saints for Now*. New York: Sheed & Ward, 1952.

Lappin, Peter. *Give Me Souls! Life of Don Bosco*. Huntington, IN: Our Sunday Visitor, 1977.

The Legend and Writings of Saint Clare of Assisi. Saint Bonaventure, NY: The Franciscan Institute, 1953.

McGinley, Phyllis. *Saint-Watching*. New York: The Viking Press, 1969.

Merton, Thomas. *What Are These Wounds?* (Life of Saint Lutgarde of Aywières). Milwaukee, WI: The Bruce Publishing Company, 1950.

Montalembert, Count de. *The Life of Saint Elizabeth*. New York: P. J. Kennedy & Sons, n.d.

Musurillo, Herbert, ed. *The Acts of the Christian Martyrs*. Oxford: Oxford University Press, 1972.

Newcomb, James F. *Saint Theresa Margaret of the Sacred Heart of Jesus*. New York: Benziger Brothers, 1934.

The Paradise or Garden of the Holy Fathers. Translated by A. Wallis Budge. Seattle, WA: Saint Nectarios Press, 1978.

Purcell, Mary. *Don Francisco: The Story of Saint Francis Xavier*. Westminster, MD: The Newman Press, 1954.

Peers, E. Allison, ed. *The Life of Teresa of Jesus*. Garden City, NY: Image Books, 1960.

Purcell, Mary. *Saint Anthony and His Times*. New York: Hanover House, 1960.

Raymond of Capua. *The Life of Saint Catherine of Siena*. New York: P. J. Kennedy & Sons, 1960.

Sackville-West, V. *Saint Joan of Arc*. New York: The Literary Guild, 1936.

Sheed, F. J., ed. *Saints Are Not Sad*. New York: Sheed & Ward, 1949.

Simi, Gino J., and Mario M Segreti. *Saint Francis of Paola*. Rockford, IL: Tan Books and Publishers, Inc., 1977.

Simpson, Gertrude, and W. Sparrow Simpson, eds. *The Life and Legend of Saint Vedast*. London: privately published, 1896.

Thomas of Celano. *Saint Francis of Assisi. First and Second Life of Saint Francis*, Translated by Placid Hermann, O.F.M. Chicago: Franciscan Herald Press, 1963.

Thurston, Herbert, S. J., and Donald Attwater, eds. *Butler's Lives of the Saints* (4 vols.). Westminster, MD: Christian Classics, Inc., 1956.

Vicaire, M. H., O. P. *Saint Dominic and His Times*. New York: McGraw-Hill Book Company, 1964.

Ward, Maisie. *Saints Who Made History: The First Five Centuries*. New York: Sheed and Ward, Inc., 1959.

Watkin, E. E. *Neglected Saints*. New York: Sheed & Ward, 1955.

Glossary

Abbot—a man who is head of an abbey of monks.

Albigenses—a religious sect, based in southern France during late 12th and early 13th century; taught a dualism, affirming two eternal principles of good and evil.

Benedictine Rule—a pattern of life developed in 540 by Saint Benedict of Nursia for his monks and used by numerous religious communities of men and women throughout the Middle Ages.

Blessed—a title applied to a person whom the Roman Catholic Church allows to be recognized as worthy of being imitated.

Canon—a member of a clerical group living according to a canon or rule; a clergyman serving in a cathedral or collegiate church.

Carmelite Order—the Order of Our Lady of Mount Carmel, founded in the 12th century in Palestine; Carmelite communities of men and women spread throughout Europe in the 13th and 14th centuries.

Capuchins—offshoot of the Friars Minor founded in 1552 in order to return to the primitive simplicity of the order.

Catechist—a person who instructs others in Christian doctrine.

Catechumen—a person who is receiving instruction in basic Christianity in preparation for baptism.

Cathari—a dualist sect that was prominent in 12th-century Germany; its adherents in France and Italy were called Albigenses or Albigensians.

Chapter—an assembly or meeting of the canons of a cathedral.

Cîteaux—the central house of the Cistercian Order, a strict Benedictine monastic community founded in the 11th century.

Diocese—the district under a bishop's supervision.

Doctor of the church—a title given to Christian theologians of outstanding merit and acknowledged saintliness.

Eucharist—Mass, the Lord's Supper, or Holy Communion; the name of the central act of Christian worship.

Fathers of the church—early Christian authors whose authority on doctrinal matters carried special weight.

Faculty, faculties—license by a church authority to perform a function or hold an ecclesial office.

Friars Minor—the religious community of men founded by Saint Francis of Assisi in the 13th century.

Friars Preachers—the religious community of men founded by Saint Dominic in the 13th century.

Host—the consecrated bread of the Eucharist.

Lent—penitential season observed in preparation for Easter.

Mitre—a tall, ornamented cap with peaks in front and back, worn by abbots, bishops, and popes as a sign of their office.

Novice—a person on probation in a religious group before taking vows.

Novitiate—the training program for new members of religious orders.

Order—a religious community of men or women who live according to a rule of life.

Papacy—the term used for the government or office of the pope.

Prior—the second in command under an abbot in a monastery; the head of a priory, a subordinate unit of a monastery.

Provincial—the governor of a province, a geographical unit of a religious order.

Religious—a man or woman who belongs to a religious order.

Religious order—a community of men or women who are committed to live according to a rule of life.

Spiritual director—a pastor or counselor who governs the Christian life of another person.

Tertiary—a member of a Third Order, an association of laymen or laywomen who pattern their lives on the rule of a religious community, but who continue to live ordinary secular lives.

We want to hear from you. Please send your comments about this book to us in care of the address below. Thank you.

ZondervanPublishingHouse
Grand Rapids, Michigan 49530
http://www.zondervan.com

We want to hear from you. Please send your comments about this book to us in care of the address below. Thank you.

ZondervanPublishingHouse
Grand Rapids, Michigan 49530
http://www.zondervan.com